# From Desperation to Preparation Comes Transformation

## *"Wisdom in Transformation"*
## Volume Two

Elder Gwendolyn Corbitt Conedy

Author's Tranquility Press
ATLANTA, GEORGIA

Elder Gwendolyn Corbitt Conedy/Author's Tranquility Press
3900 N Commerce Dr. Suite 300 #1255
Atlanta, GA 30331, USA
www.authorstranquilitypress.com

Ordering Information:
Quantity sales. Special discounts are available on quantity purchases by corporations, associations, and others. For details, contact the "Special Sales Department" at the address above.

From Desperation to Preparation Comes Transformation/ Elder Gwendolyn Corbitt Conedy
Paperback: 978-1-964037-09-7
eBook: 978-1-964037-10-3

# CONTENTS

## PART ONE

## PART TWO

## PART THREE

To everyone who encouraged me to never give up, but to stay focused on my story, and my testimony. All my Christian Minister Circle of Women, in California, who prayed for me during my struggle.

To my dearly beloved, Father and Mother, the Late Deacon and Deaconess, Ralph, and Alethia Corbitt Sr. and my immediate and extended family, in New Jersey and California.

My Darling Son, George Corvelle Conedy and his beautiful wife, Jacquelyn Conedy.

Those Who prayed me through for most of my years, but never had the opportunity to experience all my 40 years of life in California, how God prepared and transformed my life for His Purpose and His Kingdom.

To God Be the Glory

Thank you!

*We, humans, keep brainstorming options and plans, But GOD'S purpose prevails. Proverbs 19:21 (MSG)*

*We can make many plans, but the LORD'S purpose will prevail. Proverbs 19:21 (NLT)*

*Many plans are in a man's heart, but the Lord's decree will prevail. Proverbs 19:21 (NIV)*

*There are Many plans in a man's heart, Nevertheless, the LORD'S counsel-that will stand. Prov. 19:21 (NKJ)*

# From Desperation To Preparation Comes Transformation

"I CAN DO ALL THINGS THROUGH CHRIST WHO GIVES ME THE STRENGTHENS" Phil.4:13"

"AND MY GOD SHALL SUPPLY ALL MY NEEDS

ACCORDING TO HIS RICHES IN GLORY BY CHRIST

JESUS" Phil. 4:19

"WE KNOW THAT ALL THINGS WORK TOGETHER[A] FOR THE GOOD OF THOSE WHO LOVE GOD, WHO ARE CALLED ACCORDING TO HIS PURPOSE."
Romans 8:28

It is necessary to share with you before I move forward this portion of my book.

My experiences in my Forty years (40) in California I believe were my *preparation* for a greater work in the Kingdom God had to relocate me away from my birthplace, localities, people, and places of familiarity. I pray this will be of help to someone if no more than strengthen you in your walk and not be ashamed to tell your story at the appointed time which is God's timing.

# Part One
# Preparation

# Introduction

In the book "CELEBRATION OF DISCIPLINE"
by Richard J. Foster,

Donald Coggan Quotes:

"I go through life as a transient on my way to eternity, made in the image of God, but with that image debased, needing to be taught how to meditate, to worship, and to think."

I was going in my direction, moving away from God, in my own world just as "Donald Coggan" mentions in his quote, as a (transient) moving from place to place in California, not knowing who I was, what I was and where I was going it was to an eternity hell, just having fun in skin my flesh.

Yes, I was made in the image of God according to Genesis 1:27, (So God created mankind in the image of God) to do His will and not my will, But I fell out of the will of God, (perfect will into His permissive will) and almost in a turnaround of my life into a (reprobated mind) thought I lost my position in Christ, my worth, my value, and my dignity. BUT GOD knew what I needed and that was. "To be taught how to meditate, to worship, and to think...." Like God, returning to Him, LEAD TO MY TRANSFORMATION.

# Introduction: Volume Two

Enduring many sleepless nights in the process of writing and contemplating, how to begin as thoughts occurred in my mind, not wanting to expose too much, and being guided by my thoughts, knowing my story and experiences, surely would be real and help someone. What came to my mind, as I pondered, who would be interested in sitting down and reading about my life and my 40-year transition? Well through much prayer it was inevitable that it would be life-changing, helpful, encouraging and transforming of the mind. The excitement was in my spirit for someone to know, how God will and transform my life, all for His good, and purpose. Just an encouraging word, he will certainly do the same for someone who is reading this book.

*"For there is no respect of persons with God"* Rom. 2:11

He loves us with an Everlasting love.

On the contrary yes, there will be others with judgmental spirits and differences of opinion, but it's all good with God.

You see before my transition, even though' I was a born-again believer, loved the Lord, god-fearing young lady, raised in a Christian home, baptized in water, and worked in the church as a Church Pianist, and Sunday school teacher, all because of Christ, HIS Grace, and Mercy, His plan and purpose for my life. Having no knowledge, as an imperfect human being. Living a life with so many flaws, and covering up with my materialistic living, going through turmoil, trying to live by other people standards, and making grandiose mistakes, God still loved me and had Mercy on my life.

To God Be the Glory, who sent His son, Jesus to die for me, looking beyond my faults, when everyone judged my faults, and He saw my need for a Savior even during my time of a messy life. It was nothing of my own or any contributions made on my behalf. It was all the Lord's doing, his creation, with no carbon copy, and so glad man had nothing to do with it, I might have been wiped out. It is Marvelous in my sight.

Most of my experiences, as you read were my transition to New York, *desperate to* live on my own where my backsliding behavior began living a sinful life, then to return back home to Pleasantville, to become the church musician, anticipating to live the nice church girl, during those few years at home, cooperating with my parents, complying to the rules of the house, but rebelling to the situations confront me. Yes, I was a rebellious young church girl, but then I decided it was time for a change, a big change, my plans were to move and California, help my brother with his family and come back home. but since we found our uncle's family there, I decided to make a living in sunny California, had no idea God was in the planning, preparation, and transformation business for me. It was a 40-year journey *in preparation for transformation* partly in a backslidden, sinful, dark, substance abuse, drug addiction, homeless, life and how God *delivered me, into transformed my life, to His Masterpiece.* You will read later in the pages of this Volume II my return home to Pleasantville as a product of how God transformed my life, the process, ready to walk in my divine purpose, with a divine calling God prepared for me from the beginning while I was in my mother's womb.

There were trips away, too many women's conferences, Revivals, Fasting, Praying, shut-in training, workshops, much counseling, and people who ministered and taught me how to live as a woman of excellence and what was necessary at that time for my life.

Meeting many women of God serious about ministry, who love the Lord, who worked full time in Ministry, Women of God, Evangelist, Pastors, who cared about my soul, continued to pray with me, just real Women and Men of God, but I was just rebellious and uninterested in the spiritual conversation, not ready to give up and give in, it was never activated nor registered, in my spirit, during that time. but they continued to pray for me in my state of confusion until God opened my heart to hear what He sent them to do.

Women who knew of my *desperation*, just be me and yield to the flesh and what it craved. I was consoled by friends until the time of *preparation*, and I was spiritually ready to move into my *Transformation* life. Many times, my heart was ready, but my body and mind and flesh had to get ready. My decisions were to experience on my own, in desperation to move forward in life as I pleased, on own, never wanted to be a follower, always a leader, evidently this was the Lord imparting His spirit, sending his women of God to teach me leadership for his purpose, but not aware at the time surely on my journey it was inevitable and destine to be my testimony later down the road, to reach other women, struggling, in crisis, as they lead in the church with the love of God in their hearts.

Being inspired by friends, co-workers, Ministers, Pastors, Evangelists who knew me (before and after my transition) and of course, the Holy Spirit, in my late hours and time encouraged me to write, but I would start and stop, put the manuscript down, procrastinate, give up, But it entered in my spirit someone may experience, or going through the same if not a similar testimony. I pray and hope this will be an encouraging moment for the reader or someone you may share, and then maybe you.

This is my Testimony, My Story of 40 years in Los Angeles, California

# My Transition from Pleasantville NJ to
# Los Angeles, California

*THERE'S NO STORM THAT GOD*

*WON'T CARRY YOU THROUGH*

*NO BRIDGE THAT*

*GOD WON'T HELP YOU CROSS.*

*NO BATTLE THAT*

*GOD WON'T HELP YOU WIN.*

*TRUST GOD AND NEVER GIVE UP.*

AMEN

Writer anonymous

# Introduction of Volume Two
## PART ONE

In continuation of my first Volume of "My Story" you must understand, that I will be very transparent in sharing throughout the book as you will recognize because this is my purpose for writing if I cannot be real and truthful, it will not be a true story of my life and encouragement or helpful to someone struggling in life in their own flesh even in their walk with the Lord, So, at the beginning of my *preparation*, I did not have a relationship with the Lord Jesus Christ, of course, so much like many of us in our early church years, I was baptized, in water, as my momma would say:

"I went down as a dry devil and came up as a wet devil" not really but that's what the Older Saints (season Christians) would say to us when we were mischievous in church and in our ways, (flesh) I love the church activities, did not really know the lord or had knowledge of salvation and being born again. The songs we sang growing up were joyful and made you happy and glad. Should I say just love going to rehearsals and engaging in church stuff. Most of all, enjoyed every bit of church fellowship of course my friends, which made me a good Church Girl such as:

- Playing the piano (Church Musician)

- Sing in the Church

- A choir director

- Sunday school teacher

- Usher (when necessary)

- Bethany Baptist Young People's Association

- Church trips as a Delegate

And all in the same church since I was 9 years of age, as far as I can remember, for years until I graduated from High School in 1963. I really enjoyed my church friends and family., you know how you go to church for fun at that time. But it was time for a change of life as it became very boring at the time because you see I was doing it for the sake of my parents.

When you are raised in a Christian home and atmosphere, and when your Father is Chairman of the Deacon Board, and your Mother a Deaconess in the Baptist Church, you bet you will be in church every time the church door opens and all day long, morning service, afternoon service and most of the time evening something going on in Community Baptist Church. Deacon Ralph Corbitt Sr. (my daddy) whenever he put the key in the door and opened it, we were there with him, well not all the time because he had chores to do at the church as Chairman of the deacon board., while mom would go to her deaconess meetings of course she also had duties. But on Sunday she would come alone later, if she came at all, don't get me wrong Mom would make sure all the children were up and out before she could get ready, except the first Sunday. Mom had all of us dressed, made sure we had breakfast and sometimes helped Daddy, which tired her out. You see I looked at the part, dressed the part, played the part, but there was a part in my heart, a void missing but never understood what I really needed to fill the void.

For the most part, I really had the desire to move away but never had the nerve or the guts to move away from my family and church. Told you I was a "church girl" and a daddy's girl.

Many times, I had mistaken my feelings, emotions and activities, with my relationship with the Lord, by this, I mean yes, we were forced to attend church, as I was told, as they said, of course, we were raised in the church house, this is exactly what we happened, we join the church but not God. It was never taught to me concerning my relationship or salvation, well, maybe I did not understand, because my mind was on other things, and as I grew older realizing it was all emotions, and feelings of my own flesh, and trying to appease and please my parents in the church thing, all for my parents. I learned how to do things in the church, and sometimes I was forced to do the church things, events, and activities most of the time, but my behavior was almost perfect. something like, *learned behavior?* growing up in a Christian home? It was all to please my parents and the people in the church. Don't get me wrong, I enjoyed what I was doing but it was for all the wrong purpose, or reason, some of your reading this book, and know you can relate to my testimony.

So please keep an open mind and an open heart to understand my story, we all have a story to share, but this is My Story to share with you, hopefully, this will help someone, some young person or someone do not know who they are in the Lord but trying to be understanding your life in this season.

# Chapter One
# Preparation
# Prep-a-ra-tion

The action or process of making ready or being made ready for use or consideration.

"The best preparation for tomorrow is doing your best today." - H. Jackson Brown Jr.

"Education is not preparation for life, education is life itself." - John Dewey

"You must rely on your preparation. You must really be passionate and try to prepare more than anyone else and put yourself in a position to succeed, and when the moment comes.

You must enjoy, relax, breathe, and rely on your preparation so that you can perform and not be anxious or filled with doubt." -Steve Nash

Continuing from my first book, after graduation in 1963, from Pleasantville High School, it was an enjoyable summer vacation, with all my graduate friends and lady friends having a good time enjoyment and when I say a good time, it was just that. Well, there was nothing left in the wooded area of Pleasantville New Jersey but to work, go to church, go out on weekends.

I was still living at home with my parents, enjoying a single life and not feeling intimidated, being judged, and misjudged by people. Enjoying friends, relatives, those with the same mind makes a difference when you are at this age of seeking real life friends. But there was that fear or feeling of leaving my parents and likewise parents did not want me to move away from home. So, I would commute from New York back home and to Philadelphia and back home, this was the lifestyle now. just enjoying life or I should say experiencing me, myself, and I with the freedom outside the church activities. (Trying to find myself) Had my own car, well my daddy's car, a good job, dressed well, looked good, (got that from momma) and I had no plans of moving out the house, no time soon, at least that was my intention at this time in my life. I really wanted to stay and help Momma and Daddy, since I had my job and driving daddy's car, of course taking Mom where she needed to go, of course, there was no need to drive to church it was across the street, but I love my parents dearly.

So, all my friends decided to move away from home, sometimes we feel the need to grow up on our own, without the help of our parents by moving out the house, you know how we just feel grown not living in our parents' home, go in and out at our leisure, but respecting the home at the same time.

My mind began to flip flop on where, what, was next move and my decision that was exciting for me. God always have plans for us, and growing up in the church we feel a twixt in our little mind what we want but not what God desires. Well, one of my girlfriends moved to Africa, which was out of the picture, of course she married there. Then my other girlfriend lives in New York, I been there, done that, and my other Girlfriend live in the Virgin Island that sound refreshing but not hitting a nerve.

So, I tried to wait on the Lord, not knowing He was birthing something in my spirit that I did not understand, because really, I thought it was my doing. You know when you travel sometimes or go places and you think it's all you, but, no, no, its ALL GOD'S

DOING. Taking you through the process, and you enjoy the process your way.

# Chapter Two
## Preparation for Purpose

Sometime later part of 1967 we received a call from my brothers, James, my (oldest brother) and my (deceased brother) Ralph Jr. who were stationed in the navy base in Long Beach, California. They had located our relatives, my mother's brother-in-law, her deceased sister's husband, and family. This was exciting news, because we had never met our cousins ever in life before, only pictures of them when they were 2,3,4 years of age. My mom was family oriented, LOVE, LOVE, LOVE, FAMILY, and always kept pictures of family around the house so that we would always remember family far and near.

So later in the year. James was discharged from the Navy; his time was up, and it was time to return home. Ralph Jr. had to remain until discharged. He and his family remained in California, which helped me to make up my mind and decide for my journey to California and help my brother and sister-in-law with the children, (really babies) as he would have to report for duty on the ship for months at a time.

Yes, it was most definitely my desire, not knowing God's other plans, during my stay in California, for my life, and orchestrating all the time. Yes, because as you read further in the book you will see, THE TRANSFORMATION in my life as I picture, God's hand moving upon my life, just as the Holy Spirit moved upon the earth in Genesis, if I can put it in this way:

In the beginning, God created. (*Gwendolyn Corbitt*) the heavens and the earth.

Now the earth (*Gwendolyn*) was formless and empty, darkness covered (Gwendolyn) the surface of the watery depths, and the Spirit of the surface God was hovering over (Gwendolyn) GET THE PICTURE.

*"We may make our plans, but God has the last word. You may think everything you do is right, but the Lord judges your motives"*
*Proverbs 16:1-2 ESV.*

I began to think outside the box, to live a life outside of Christian teaching ignoring momma and daddy's teacher and how I was raised, you know when we reach a certain age, for many of us raised in a Christian home, we often say, "I'm grown" and want to branch out "feel our oats" smelling ourselves. Well, that's what Gwen begins to do. Making decisions, choices, of course, while making my own money" and it felt good about this new thing. I am now ready to embark upon, a new thing in my life although' I had the fear of God but was not afraid of the world. I just felt He (God) had His hands on me due to the seed that was planted from birth and for many years of praying mother and father.

God began to prepare me for something I could not handle at the present time. So, he had to move me away from all the noisome pestilence, all the distractions, that was in my life, all the mess, all my surroundings of negativity. The worldly platforms, and traps the enemy set for me, in the opposite direction of God's plans for my life.

This was really stepping outside the box unfamiliar place, but many familiarities, different people. There would be some to speak in my life, to lead me on the right path for Ministry, to begin my Transformation but I rejected.

*For I know the plans I have for you, declares the LORD, plans for welfare and not for evil to give you a future and hope. -Jeremiah 29:11*

I was unaware of so much darkness in my life at the time and if I remained in Atlantic City, and Pleasantville my life would have been a disaster and going against the plans of God. I was making a mess of my life, heading into a world of destruction and disaster, into the enemy's territory without the proper spiritual clothes ready to be wiped out by the Devil. He was trying to take control, and yes, raised in a Christian Home, baptized with water, working in the church, I still did not truly know the Lord, nor did I allow Him to take control of my life, to walk in His, Perfect will, instead I walked in His permissive will, because I did not know the difference.

Did I know my purpose? No

Did I know the will of God for my life? (Perfect will)

No

Did I even know myself? The area I wanted to know.

We can walk around for years, attending church, bible study, church meetings, singing in the choir, working in the usher board, just going through the motions, serving and have no knowledge of our purpose or God's Perfect will for our lives, walking in His permissive will, unaware. There is a difference.

**Permissive** will: It may not be God's will, but He will permit us to do it because He loves us.

**Perfect** Will: He speaks, gives us directions and we obey. I became a man-pleaser, pleasing and chasing after the flesh and not after God, as I did for years, being destroyed by the devil unaware. You see we know our inner man is crying out while the flesh is being satisfied.

*"The Devil comes only to steal and kill and destroy...." John 10;10*

An opportunity presented and I decided to leave on my own. Ready but spiritually unprepared to move into another place, a new home and yet so far away from home, my time was up on the East Coast and ready to make a New Start on the West Coast. Well at least that was my thoughts at the present time, But God was really behind the scenes, orchestrating the move. We make the plans, but God intervenes and interrupt at His time.

You will see how God continue to use me for His Glory. When God has your life in His hand nothing can pluck you out.

The bible says: in John 10:9 "I give my sheep eternal life. They will never die, and no one can take them out of my hand."

You will read later in the book how I almost died in my sins, But God had plans for my life, and He would receive the Glory, as the Devil had a Plot. It wasn't until I began to Read, and Study the word, for myself, not just Study but digest it making it applicable to my life. Then fell in love with the Lord and developed an intimate relationship with Him and not man.

"Falling in love with Jesus, was the best thing I ever done."

It was not until the Lord revealed himself to me during a time in my life, in my stupor, almost dying from a drug overdose, unreal? Well, this is real, this church girl's life, was over, but, God spared, my life so many times for His purpose.

*"All things worked together for my good, because I love the Lord, and it was according to His purpose, Roman 8:28*

"Preparation to Transformation began."

# A Made-up Mind with a Confused Heart

*"Prayer is the cure for a confused mind a weary soul, and a broken heart."*

*"An unsettled mind is a sign of an unsettled spirit." -unknown.*

*"For God is not the author of confusion, but of peace."*
*-I Corinth 14:33*

# preparation for purpose, made up mind continues

*"Therefore, prepare your mind for action, keep sober in spirit, and fix your hope completely on the grace to be brought to you at the revelation."1 Peter 1:13*

Looking back over my life, a song enters my spirit, I used to sing.

"As I look back over my life, and I think things OVER, I can truly say that God has made a way, I have a TES-TI -MO-NY"

Yes, my entire life is a testimony, so many tests, trials, and experiences but God brought me through it all. That was another song:

"Through it all, through it all,

I've learned to trust in Jesus, I've learned to trust in God, Through it all, Through it all,

I've learned to depend upon His Word."

There was a little unfinished business, and relationships, which needed closure, but at the time, it never entered my mind. You see, I did not fully understand because of was confused in my heart, not concerned, unsettled in my spirit, but desired peace of mind and not knowing how to receive it or where to start. As I pondered over and over to relocate, I sat down to really look over my life. As I realized later, had I not taken the opportunity at the time of my compiling all my thoughts and gathering data from my brain, and my heart, or as we say, moving on that first mind but really the holy spirit nudging me, prompting me at the right time, I might not have been here today to Share "MY STORY". But no one knows like God and the Holy Spirit.

GOD is so faithful with His plans.

*"See I am doing a new thing, now it springs up; do you not perceive it." Isaiah 43:19*

*"For I know the plans I have for you," declares the Lord, "plans to prosper you and not to harm you, plans to give you hope and a future." Jeremiah 29:11*

And yes, I perceive it ready in my spirit, although I had all intentions to prosper on my own in my own flesh as it was speaking to my spirit to get out and get away right now do not procrastinate.

You see, right after I relocated there was a phone call that my best friend, running buddy, we got in trouble together, sang in the choir, ushered, and in youth bible study, my church friend, not to mention her name) died from an overdose of drugs. Can you imagine how it shook my ever-most being? unbelievable and denying it for perhaps a week, trying to pull myself together after reminiscing on the times we spent together, inside the church singing in the choir, on the usher board and outside the church, traveling on church trips, the activities we were involved and experience together no one had any idea what took place in our lives, but our Parents and sometimes they did not have knowledge, of how lost we were because we were

**"Church Girls"** trying to please our parents and the Church Folk.

I had much procrastination, confusion, immorality, sin, depression, and unhappiness, which played a big part during my church life which no one knew but my inner circle, (church sisters and brothers and friends outside the church)

In my journey, you will notice the different struggles as a **"CHURCH GIRL GONE WILD"** moving through life and how GOD used my life experiences for his glory, to accomplish HIS

PURPOSE regardless of all my difficulties, immoralities sinful nature, toxic relationships, hurt, pain, and the miss judgement of other people.

"THROUGH MY DESPERATION GOD PREPARED ME FOR MY TRANSFORMATION."

In the midst of my situation, and my messed-up life, even when your friends, family and loved ones and those around you do not understand the TRANSFORMATION, nor do they understand how Gods hands were on my life as He told me into a vessel of honor and for his glory.

*"He shall be a vessel unto honor, sanctified and meet for the master's use, and prepared unto every good work" I Tim. 20:21.*

YES, this was me, but people begin to place a title, label and try to define me according to their eyes out of ignorance we know how church folks do in their flesh, BUT GOD, placed a desire in my heart to seek him, and search for him, and begin to serve him with my whole heart. Well, there was too much more I had to experience on my own. Although the seed was planted, now someone will come along to water, and then God will give the increase in my life. But I had to delight myself in him, and that was far from my confused, unsettled mind. I was not ready currently, I am now on my own, and there was too much ahead to adventure.

*"Take delight in the Lord, and he will give you the desires of your heart." Psalm 37:4 (NIV)*

Sometimes we interpret the scriptures how we perceive it to be from a carnal perspective, because our heart belong to God and the desire of our heart must be His desire and His will for our lives. But God had a way of moving me into my destiny here on earth, unaware, even in my rebellious state, as I began moving by my fleshly desires, emotions, doing it my way, how, when and it was not by His Spirit, but by that spirit in me.

I had a made-up mind but a confused spirit, you know how you really want to do right, even though you are grown on your own, well that was my heart desire, still trying to live as my parents raised me. But as Paul, in the bible say: *every time you try to do right evil is always lurking around to pull you into the opposite way of living. Going against the grain.*

# Chapter Three
## My Anticipation in my Dream State

As I stated in Chapter one receiving a phone call that my brother had located my cousins, in Los Angeles

California, so, by this time in my life, I anticipated a great move forward to a better lifestyle, moving to the Great State of California, my dream State, where I've always dreamed of moving, part of my bucket list. Anticipating new relationships, new church, new people and hopefully marriage and building a family. You know when you hear so much about Hollywood, Movie Stars, Hills, Mountains, Valleys, bright lights, and Big City, etc. as seen in the movies I thought this was it. Looking forward to sharing my gifts and talents also, with others to experience different things in the music field which came later as my mind turned and churned like a little girl all the excitement was all around me.

You know how everyone wants the opportunity to really see Hollywood, Movie Stars, as they appear on television, with all the artistic, talented, people, yes one day expecting to be discovered by some of the theatrical Producers, songwriters, well you know, we dream and sometimes have great thoughts and ideas in our head of what and where we would like to appear, of course, I was in the right place with so much excitement in the air and jittery in my bones, with a little of anxiety and great anticipation of who, what, when, and where the new people would show up, or meet, my shining Knight Armor" come in on his white stallion horse and wipe me off my feet, of course, I can dream, this was concerning marriage relationships of course. Well, my flesh began to rise, as my mom would say: "you smellin yourself" or "you are too fresh" and that I was, my mind was on learning more about this State called California that had been waiting to explore.

Finally, my dream became realty, therefore, I believe it was in God's plan.

So, there was a phone call from my brother James before he was discharged, from the Military in Long Beach, California, but my brother Ralph was still in the Navy. So, it was good news this time, he had located our cousins whom we'd never met, who lived there in Los Angeles. My mother's nieces and nephews whom she hadn't seen since her sister's funeral. I remember so well when my mother left for California to attend her sisters' funeral, I really did not want her to go alone but, she was in good hands, and my daddy stayed behind to watch the children who watch themselves if you know what I mean.

You see Daddy was a nice daddy, for the girls, everything was. "okay" and "yes" for the girls but the boys, and Deep Noooo!!!

When momma is away the children will play and play and play. Daddy had much business in the church as Chairman of the Deacon board he was terribly busy also he cleaned the church and made sure the doors were open and close after every event at the time.

So, getting back to the fact that my cousins were located was good news, and time for a grand reunion, and celebration although it was a tragedy that had occurred. Of course, this was years after, and now they were teenagers or a little older now.

However, we were excited to hear the good news but sad we never had the opportunity to meet our Auntie, but he had the opportunity to meet the one who gave him the name Jimmy, our Uncle Jimmy, and the family at that time. Such excitement in the atmosphere to hear he my brother had met my first cousins, for the first time ever.

You see my mother had pictures of them but never had the opportunity of sharing the same space with them in the same room, in my dream State, City, Los Angeles, Calif. where I plan on living, not knowing how long.

Sad to say, that my cousin, Janice, transitioned before the completion of my first book, but the opportunity to share with my other cousins Cheri, and Gerald. Although it was a joy to see Janice and her husband, not knowing it would be the last time for both, such a loving couple. It was a great visit, she was in good spirits on my vacation, in July of 2019, before the Pandemic she transitioned to in Oct. of 2019.

Normally we would all get together on my vacation, at some one's home and talk about the good times in the 60's or my first time arriving in California, and learning how to pronounce certain streets correctly, it took a moment but we learned a new street every year and the correct pronunciation as my cousins and family enjoyed making fun of the East Coast accent, which it never dawn on me there was a NJ accent but yes, I suppose living so close to New York and Connecticut our speech was a little different to most Californians. This was an exciting moment for me, preparing to move into a new Place, new experiences, new family, and expectations of exciting new life...

Now it is time for the big move. First time for everything.

First time on a plane

First time meeting my California Family

First time moving far away from my family.

First time in the State of California.

So, there were mixed emotions settling in my spirit and all the time praying for peace, tranquility, safe traveling as I look forward to my future adventures or should I say one off my bucket list. Although the enemy tried to put fear in my spirit, I was not backing down, I had a made-up mind, a little confused in my spirit as the date became closer the more excited, I became greater. IT WAS CALIFORNIA HERE I COME.

# Chapter Four
# Preparation for Newness

*For we are His workmanship, created in Christ Jesus for good works,*
*which God prepared beforehand that we should walk in them.*
*Ephesians 2:10 (NASV)*

*I Peter 2:9 But you are chosen generation, a royal priesthood, a holy*
*nation, His own special people, that you may proclaim the praises of*
*Him who called you out of darkness into His marvelous light. —I*
*Peter 2:9 (NASV)*

Finally, the day was here. As I began my preparation packing things that day before, wondered how much to take at this time, or wait later to ship my clothes and items or not go at all. All this was going through and through my mind. My thoughts became clear as I waited and waited for the days to roll by and close this chapter in my life trying to encourage myself and build my spirit for the move. Racing in my mind was bright lights and a new city, new adventures, new people, new places, more to experience ready to spread my wings, and get out of New Jersey. Ready for a change in my life, people, environment, scenery, and church (later) but I really wanted to venture into a broader spectrum of my singing career. As I look back over my life, I was really moving and going for another reason other than what God had in mind, for His plans and purpose. I was looking forward to meeting and greeting my family, getting to know them and bonding with my Uncle Jimmy for the first time who I had ever met.

So here I am prepared to travel on this Big TWA BOWIE AIRLINES to another part of the world for the first time ever. From the FAR EAST COAST TO THE FAR WEST COAST. I called all my friends who remained in Pleasantville, NJ, and the other part of our extended family living in New Jersey, who were excited for me, many of them gave me monetarism gifts because I could not take too much on the plane, but money was always helpful and fit in my pocket. I did not want a party at this time too many people were fearful about me flying and my faith was not so strong I had a "grain of mustard see faith" so I really did not want to be around fearful, negative people at this time, it would have made me more fearful, so I chose not to have a party even to have friends over the day or night before my departure. This was to keep negative people in their own homes. I was not being (anti sociable) some people are happy for you, and some are not so happy for you put it just like that.

I will never forget traveling to the airport with my family, Daddy, Mom, and sister, it began to rain and then rain and then rain some more, never-ending. BUT ME? GWEN? She had a plane to board soon, but it was storming raining, thunder and lightning, (as we say) "it was raining like cats and dogs" and I mean it was pouring raining, lightening, thundering but it was not cold the weather was New Jersey hot, humid weather, and no one wanted to drive in the storm, at this time, well I did not know my way too well, driving to the Airport, and we did not have GPS or Google nor did we have a cell phone at that time there were no parkways, no expressways, just the BLACK HORSE PIKE and the WHITE HORSE PIKE leading to Philadelphia Airport.

It took us almost 1 1/2 hours, driving down the streets maybe a little longer at that time depending on traffic to get there but, we finally made it, and it stopped raining, and storming as soon as we arrived at the Philadelphia Airport the rain ceased, the thundering, ceased the weather was clear, and the sun came out. I was so happy because my parents did not drive too often, especially my mom I drove her everywhere she had to go, with the exception to church, but Daddy would drive to Pleasantville, and Atlantic City, maybe sometimes to my uncle Roberts Home in Philadelphia, not too often of course they have to use a map at that time. Looking back, it was only God's hands, and His Power in this to keep them safe and me encouraged that I would continue to move forward in the journey. But as we arrived at the airport, you were able to park your car in front at this time and walk your family upstairs, at this time of Century. So, they did just that and waited for me to board and were supposed to wait for the plane to take off. Of course, I could not see them.

I had mixed feelings, and was frightened of leaving home, going so far away from family and friends, for the first time. I will never forget my mom reminding me of the songs I sang in church "walk on by faith each day" by James Cleveland who I expected to see once I got settled in California and visited his church other songs, to keep my mind on the Lord and never look back in fear. Songs we sang but never knew what they meant as we were singing at the time, we just enjoyed what we were doing at the time. We never understood hymns, and gospel songs in the church, we were using our musical talents for the Lord.

So, as we finally arrived at the Philadelphia Airport my very first time flying, and that far away, when we arrived on time, I was not in a rush to walk down the long hall in the Philadelphia Airport which is such a long walk, but it was Lords doing, and it was all in God's hands.  The rain had ceased, and the sun was shining, although I did not see a rainbow, But, Momma and Daddy were able to see their big daughter, their second child, off to the big City of Los Angeles, Calif. Of course, they had mixed feelings, although didn't show it, and by them knowing it was family it helped them to feel a little more excited and less fearful about me leaving. I believe that it was approximately five and half hours, straight on TWA BOWIE AIRLINES 747, it was alright with our souls.  So glad mom and Dad's family were allowed to come upstairs with me to wave and kiss me off then chills began to run up and down my body, and I began to feel nervous, and of course that negativity and fear tried to take over, but I had those songs in my mind and began to Humm.... I was concerned for their safety returning home from the Airport and they also wanted to encourage me to keep going, not to fear, just trust Him, and I really believed in His spirit at that time. I believe the Lord was truly with me. But as I looked back at my family waving, goodbye, not know how to feel, happy, sad, glad, wondering will this be the last time, I would see them, and kept the songs in my head, thoughts, and prayers,

"Walk on by Faith each day."

"Lord will make a way somehow."

"God will take care of You."

"I had a talk with God last night."

YESSSS, I had a talk with him, and I prayed the night before, out of fear, so glad He understood us more than we understood and trusted Him, He knew I would arrive safely at my destination.

So, as I boarded this big 747 JET TWA BOWIE Airplane to California, I felt a little brave, bold, and excited, tried to feel like a celebrity boarding a flight for a new adventure movie, just trying to keep my spirits high and have a little joy down in my soul. All the time I was nervous, scared, but excited. I located my seat and sat down. It was a wide body meaning (8) eight seats across the aisle, so I had a row to myself, first class, but all seats were the same. (Now remember I was of age and did not have a relationship with the Lord) So, I bought myself a small glass of wine and went to sleep. It was a smooth, and comfortable five-hour ride. Well, I did not know the difference until that BIG JET landed in Los Angeles, California safely. My Dream State.

# Chapter Five
## Landing and Arriving in LAX

"SETTLING IN, "SETTLING DOWN"

Stepping off the Bowie 747 TWA Airplane in California made me feel like a new person immediately.

The song writer says "I left my heart in San Francisco" I had left everything, bad memories, most of my clothes in Pleasantville, not my heart it appeared to be a new spirit, a new season, it was a joy, looking at the tall palm trees and the weather was absolutely my dream, yes, missing my family, but I felt in my spirit this is what the Lord wanted for my life and most assuredly what I desired. You know when you move to a place of your choice, of course, your desires sometimes do not line up with God's desire, especially when you are not delighting yourself in Him as you should and leaning not to your own and understanding with so many distractions, excitement, looking forward to meeting and greeting new faces. It's nothing like a new outlook on life, starting all over again.

My late brother Ralph and his wife Bertha met me at the airport with their two babies, little Darryl, and Donna walking and one on the horizon, on the way. I was ready to experience a NEW THING, whatever there was to experience, I was ready and willing. So, we traveled on a four (4) lane freeway called the 110 Harbor Freeway, something I had never experienced but it was amazing and of course, the people were driving just like they lived there and moving as though' they knew just where they were going. Well, my brother Jr. kept up with the flow of the traffic and I did sightsee as much as I could. Riding on the freeway was so different, than riding on the black horse pike, or white horse pike, no expressways in New Jersey at the time. It was as though' I woke up to a dream come true, so emotionally excited.

It was such an EXCITEMENT finally making it to CALIFORNIA, FROM THE FAR EAST COAST TO THE FAR WEST COAST. FROM THE ATLANTIC OCEAN TO THE PACIFIC OCEAN. It was amazing new food, new sights, new housing, look like Hawaii, and Mexico. I was finally far away from my problems and situations, or so I thought, but until I developed an intimate relationship with the Lord, asking to forgive me and bringing closure to my situations, and doors left open in my life there was no moving forward for me. We never get rid of our past until we bring closure to the old and sincere about changing our lives and letting go of everything and not holding anything in reserve.

Just as Paul said in Philippians 3: 13

*"Brothers, I do not consider that I have made it my own. But one thing I do: forgetting what lies behind and straining forward to what lies ahead I press on toward the goal for the prize of the upward call of God in Christ Jesus" (ESV)*

*"My friends, I don't feel that I have already arrived. But I forget what is behind, and I struggle for what is ahead. I run toward the goal, so that I can win the prize of being called to heaven. This is the prize that God offers because of what Christ Jesus has done." (NIV)*

My desire was to let go of my past, leave all the negativity, drama, hurt pain, and closure behind that I experienced in New Jersey and press, struggle, and strain toward the prize and plan, God had for me. Although' it was not all bad, there was some good I learned and it was time for me to leave and learn new ideas, and new people. He will take us through a process of change when we are serious about change or a transformational experience which I am sure, most of us have experienced the metamorphosis, real change in our lives. The "Damascus Road Experience" Yes, God can and will change our lives when we are sincere and ready, he will not force anything on us, it is our choice, to live a life of happiness, or turmoil, drama and unhappiness, seesaw, roller coaster lifestyle, doing whatever we desire, when we desire and with whoever we desire regardless of our home training, "we are loose as a goose" grown as and ponytail, and hot and fired up ready to go.

I moved to California with my younger brother, Ralph Jr. (who is now deceased) and his wife, with their three babies, because his sweet wife needed help, as a navy wife. They were so in love and enjoyed family life and increasing the fruit population of having children although' the bible says, "be fruitful and multiply" they were doing their part on the earth. It appeared every time his ship went out to sea, she was left to nurture and care for the babies alone, this was no easy task or assignment for her since they were nine months apart. I can remember many times, we waved him off on the ship, praying for his return in a month, we never knew what to expect, as the sailors sat on the ship in the middle of the Pacific Ocean for a month or two or three or even maybe six months, to a year. Which was a long time in military training.

Then upon his return, it was exciting to see him pull in on this huge ship with all the other sailor's families waiting on the deck and how they salute together as they exit the ship with the military band and flags waving overly exciting new experience for me to witness.

After my brother returned home of course there was a party going on in the Corbitt's household and sharing all his activities, during his time on the ship, living on the water, in the middle of the Pacific Ocean.

Many times, the Chief or Captain would open the doors for all the families and friends to board the ship for a family and friends activity day, this was quite an experience with excitement and fun. There were so many people to meet. I have been on airplanes, and now an opportunity to experience a Huge Ship, large enough to carry many helicopters. I think the name was called "KERSARGE" out of Long Beach, California, just to ride there for a day was exciting to me, because this was my first time in California and then Long Beach right at the Pacific Ocean, such a pretty, beautiful sky-blue Ocean. Also, there was an amusement park there, like the boardwalk in Atlantic City but, it was as though' we were walking on the walk, with amusement rides, etc. there in Long Beach. The beach was just as clean and pretty, the sand had a sandy color, with a smooth touch to your hands and feet, it was lovely just to walk in the sand with no shoes letting the sand roll between your toes.

We would pack lunch and have a nice picnic on the beach in the smooth sand blankets for all the children and whoever was the baby at that time, umbrella and/or chaise. And let the fun excitement begin. Now this was the cleanest beach in this area. There were others, but some were not so clean, however, he took us to the best for the betterment of the children. I thought all the beaches in California were beautiful, you would think. But by him as one in the Navy, brother knew best for his family. I would buy a new bathing suit at this time it was a two-piece bikini, oh yea, my new recreation for me and exciting, the weather was right, and I was ready for some excitement. Of course, Anxiety with excitement was settling in my spirit at this time, not knowing what to expect, or who I will meet. But my brother was a little over baring with me, (overprotective) although I was the oldest, watching me closely, not that I was going anywhere because I was in a strange land with strange people, not really but, Gwendolyn, did not want to get lost so soon.

Settling Down in California was so exciting for me, but my mother's excitement was.

"Gwen did you find a church yet?" or "stay with the Lord" or remember the songs you sang in the choir, "Walk on by faith each day" and all the other songs."

# Chapter Six
# "Searching for a Church"
# (church hopn)

*"Trust in the Lord with all your heart and lean not to your own understanding in all your ways acknowledge Him and He will direct your path. "Proverbs 3:5-6*

Finally in the State of California, my dream State, and part of my bucket list contemplating living here forever, meeting new friends, and family and maybe husband of course seeking occupation.

I lived with my brother in a community that appeared to be a small Community of navy men at one time could have been Navy homes, I remember my mom telling me as I left home to "make sure you find a church" not to hang in the streets too long without being in church. So, in this Community was a little small Family Pentecostal Church I frequently attended.

Enjoyed the spirit of the people, and service, although' the Pastor was a little long-winded, well, I thought he was because coming from a Baptist church where we wanted to be ("Bapti'costal") aa mixture of emotions and feelings, during the singing but when the preacher began to preach and the people began to fall asleep, he knew when to say his last words. We were trying to be joyous, happy, and holy Ghost but, well you know what I'm talking about, so nevertheless it was the only church that reminded us of home church. I had visited others not too far away, but it was international and interracial, something I was not too familiar with. So, first things first, to satisfy my parents, again, especially my mother, I began to attend this community church in the complex, with my brother and his wife and family, because whenever I spoke to my mother, her conversation was about being in church, yes, of course, that was her interest first. So even if I did not join a church as we say, or attend too often on my mom's next phone call, my answer would be,

"I'm still looking mom,"

"I'm still searching Mom."

"But not yet."

So, I continued to stay with my brother in his house, City called Harbor City, California, for a few years, their complex of Harbor City, California, where there were nice shiny, hard wooden floors, two story, nice greenery back yard for the children to play, not far from the beach area, until I was able to get on my feet, find a job to help with finances. But of course, he wanted me to stay and help with the family during his stay on the ship.

Currently, it was not a good idea for me to move at this time and leave them alone. On the other side of this it would be quite right for me but not feasible, you see he was in the Navy and Navy man in their Navy suits seem to excite me because of the neatness and how they look so slim and trim, even if they were fat, it was just something about the uniform, their discipline, mannerism, and politeness. Well, my brother did not allow me alone with any of them. (overprotected) He knew more about them than I did so that was the end of my adventure before it started. While the devil had a plot God had a PLAN.

Although, he had a few parties and I met a few with some interesting gentlemen, they were so polite and humble. Smelling good, not old spice, but expensive cologne, of course the price was discounted for them because they would buy from the Navy Ship

Store, on the base in Long Beach, Calif., nothing like a good clean, smelling, navy, gentleman, good looking, well groom man, with an intelligent conversation, and without a narcissistic personality and an Opportunistic spirit.

Although' my desire was to continue living or spending most of my life how as I desired but God had a plan which was not revealed to me yet and it surely did not include Navy Men. This began my new experience and new journey in my life. But I still did not seek to find a church and become stable. Church right now was now on my agenda. When I left it behind me it was not before me now.

It was so beautiful to meet all my cousins, and family, brother, sister-law, and their babies. It was so exciting, I did not look back contemplate on when I would return to any of my home base in New Jersey, none of that, but I did miss my New Jersey family and they were always on my mind and in my plans.

I was in a new place in my life and began to enjoy the moment I stepped off the TWA BOWIE AIRLINES in Los Angeles, California.

Arriving in California was a five-hour flight and three-hour time difference, which had to get settled in my spirit, mind, and life since this was going to be my permanent home for a while. I was prepared to stay up all night and learn about my family, a family reunion without our parents, but it was great.

The neighbors and most of the community knew my brother and he befriended most of them. He invited them over to meet us, they were very neighborly. You see my brother lived in a community where next-door neighbors shared your front and backyard, you could not build picket fences around your property, no screen door, just a hard wooden door with a small glass window. It was enough space for green grass, and a yard for the next-door neighbors and his family.

Whenever someone had a barbecue, it was enough for your family and all the neighbors, that was the love expressed to each other, as it was in the country down south everyone was all family, cousins, brothers, sisters regardless of nationality, or color. God brought everyone together. This was an interracial community near the main busy highway you dare not try to walk across. Although' we were in the midst of strangers, it appeared as if we had known each other for years.

So, I began to learn everyone in the neighborhood, well my brother Jr. was a neighborly person with an outgoing personality, and you had to become a friend or an enemy of my sweet brother, Ralph Jr. had a troubling spirit at times, quick tempered. but this was my blood brother, and you did not speak negatively concerning his family, brother, friends, or buddies even from the ship. Many did not understand his personality but learned the personality of the military brotherhood relational language. If we partied together, we were a union, came together and stayed together, like church relationship or friends but these people were real, not so much as the church folk.

I had just left behind, you see, I was bitter at this time, trying to get better, praying that God will change my heart from the bitterness about those who hurt me in church. Now I am in a new place, different environment, striving to make a better life in the excitement and time of my life.

God has a way of turning your bad into good, when it appears as though' no chance of change is in the Horizon for your good you are seeking in your life. Every time you try to do good, the enemy brings what looks good and it's all not bad and not all good either.

Paul said in Romans 8:28:

"I do not understand what I do. For what I want to do I do not do, but what I hate I do. And if I do what I do not want to do, I agree that the law is good. As it is no longer who longer I do who does it, but it is sin living in me. For I know that good itself does not dwell in me, that is in my sinful nature. For I have the desire to do what is good I want to do, but the evil I do not want to do —this I keep on doing. Now if I do what I do not want to do, it is no longer I who does it, but it is sin living in me that does it." Roman 7:5-20

*"For we know that God causes all things to work together for good to those who love God, to those who are called according to His purpose." Romans 8:28*

*As for you, you meant evil against me, but God meant it for good to bring about this present result, to preserve many people alive. "There is some Good in the worst and Some Bad in the Good." Genesis 50:20*

*My intentions were to do good, to please God first then my parents, because their spirit was still in me, they sowed good seeds in my life, and that stays with you, once the seed is planted it will grow and you cannot pluck it out, it was instilled in me for good, because my mom and daddy, did exactly what Proverbs 22:6*

"Train up their child in the way He should go and when He is old, he will not depart from IT.

The (IT) was the training of the parents instilled in their children. In those times, or era, if, I must say, "we were scared into discipline and training." We had a real Village looking after us, if we did not do the right thing, we had better do it before our parents came home or the neighbors would surely spread the fact of the matter. But it was all Good, we were a family, just as we were Neighbors in our little street, Richman Ave. New Jersey. so much for this. So, I began to use my talent and gifts in this church, by the next time my mom calls me I can share with her I am in the church playing the piano for the choir. Well, I did not become a member, just helping, obligating my time and gifts by attending every Sunday, and trying to do the right thing as much as possible. Whenever, I did not have a headache or hangover, from the night before a house party. Of course, she would not know. So, I called and shared with her,

"Hey Mom, (of course not just like that) "Guess what?

"I found a good holiness church around the corner."

"I could walk" and "I was the pianist."

Trying to make it sound good to her ears. Knowing it was not in my heart to continue as the church pianist, too much like New Jersey and I was not ready to get back in the "Church Girl thing" and did not want to mix church with Pleasure of course the Pleasure of my activities.

Of course, mom would not hear of it nor know of it, because I was not going to tell her of it, only wanted her to know the good things Gwen, her big girl, was active in at this time. Gwen was ready to get acquainted and be adventurous in this big State of CALIFORNIA so much to see and learn.

*The Lord is not slow to fulfill his promise as some count slowness, but is patient toward you, not wishing that any should perish, but that all should reach repentance. 2 Peter 3:9*

# PART TWO
## Chapter Seven
## Meeting my Los Angeles Family

Here we are finally, meeting my cousins for the very first time in my life, ever, not knowing what they were going to look like, say, or accept me, although' I've seen baby pictures of them my mom had around the house, which was sent by my Uncle Jimmy. It all sounds good on the telephone, but I could not envision them over the phone even with the pictures. So, my brother took me over to their house, in Los Angeles, a beautiful white brick stucco home, with sparkles on the outside that shined during day and night, something I've never seen before ever again that was Los Angeles, California.

There I met the entire family, my new auntie, uncle Jimmy and all my new Cousins and It was as though we met before, they greeted me, whom they never met, as their sister, not just a family member. I felt at home.

I believe they were still in School, or college and we could not stay over too late, due to the time difference we were ahead of the time, but back home, on the East Coast it was late, however, we did not make our visit too extensive at this time. My Uncle was so excited to see us, so we began to have conversations and ended up staying longer than we had anticipated. It was so exciting and loving, happiness in the air. But the night had to end, and we had to leave, it was getting late. So, the next day we were going to meet up and have dinner over at their home and stay a little longer.

Then the next day my brother drove the family out to Hollywood, Sunset Blvd. of course everyone wanted to see what Hollywood looked like, as we anticipated it to look just like TV well, we traveled down the streets due to a crowded freeway, call the 110 freeway, it was the best way to travel. So here we are on the streets of

"Hollywood and Vine" the big "Tower record" Company, and there was the "Believe it or Not."

There was one other place wanted to visit and that was Beverly Hills, where the movie stars lived, or did it make believe? We did not have time to travel up in the hills, we had a long way back down to where we were living, (South Central LA) driving day enjoyable Sunday family trip. Of course, we had more time to visit later. So, when we arrived home everyone was tired and sleepy, ready for bed, especially the babies.

We adults stayed up late again talking and having a little night cap, like a little wine and beer and whatever we wanted to drink, and eat my brother made us amazingly comfortable and welcome, well you know when family get together, we just have fun and enjoy each other. He had a 3 large bedroom and 2 story complexes.

The next morning, I was up ready to go again, but my brother planned a picnic not far by the water near the house, in (HARBOR CITY), never seen this before two blocks away was a picnic ground water and boats, canoes to ride, pony rides for the kids just a nice atmosphere. Of course, we had picnic grounds in the backyard, plenty of good room in the front OR back yard on the green grass, for the children to run around and play games, and spread a blanket out for a picnic, bring the food from the kitchen to the back or front yard. So, we did this for a little time until my brother had to pull out on the ship, and we were there alone again but not for long. During this time, he was away on the Ship, and my sister-in-law and children visited the Community Church with me, around the corner so I would be able to tell mom the truth when she called the next time.

I did attend the church a few times more, and started my routine again, playing the piano, and directing the family choir because everyone in the choir was related, many children in fact it was a family church, and the Pastor built the church himself it was large enough for everyone in the Community and more. All the children had powerful voices and loved to sing and rehearse, they just loved the church. But that was only a little while until I hooked up with my oldest cousin and returned to my old habits again. partying, well not so much of partying but they just wanted me to enjoy California since it was my first time here. I would wake up on Sunday and attend church off and on. They had a permanent Pianist, but when she was not there of course they would look for me but, I was not ready to obligate or commit myself just yet. So, I would make frequent visits so that my cousins would not get used to me too soon. You know what was next, call mom and let her know I found a church, attended and played piano when necessary. She was happy and pleased about this report and wanted to hear more about the Pastor and what denomination.

So, my girlfriend and school mate desired to come out for a while from Pleasantville to stay with me, But I would have to rent my own apartment for us to share together.

But before she came out, I met this sailor at the shore, we dated for a while and then he would go out to sea also for a while. So that would give me time to visit with my Classmate when she arrived.

# Chapter Eight
## A Fairytale Marriage

*"Do not be unequally yoked with unbelievers. For what partnership has righteousness with lawlessness? Or what fellowship has light with darkness." 2 Corinthians 6:14*

I believe it was a couple of years past or more. I went by and my brother was discharged from the Navy, and by this time I was in my own apartment around the corner from him.

So, my girlfriend is here now, and I did fine a nice apartment. close to my brother. We began to share everything. I was so happy glad to see her hadn't seen since 1967, graduation and here it was 1969. Guess what we did? Move right around the corner from him because we did not have a car at the time. We had much to chit chat about and gossip was in the chit-chat room, of course, you know how girlfriends who had seen each other for years had so much, well, just conversation. So here was my friend visiting with me, keeping me company.

But keeping the main thing the main thing. I continued to search and attend church, and although my friend was not interested at the time, we had different activities we engaged and involved in. I did introduce her to all my cousin's family. and we began to be Ladies of the night in a decent and clean way, because every time we stepped out, it was as if we stepped out of the Vogue or Mademoiselle magazine, everything matching from head to toenails if we wore a cover shoe. We were classy women of the night.

Most of our outings were Hollywood Plays or some Concerts of course parties were fun times so that was it for a long time, about 2-

3 years. We just made ourselves acquainted with the streets of California and my girlfriend is from New Jersey. He was home most of the time with his family, which was so Great for my sister-in-law and the children. Also gave me a little more freedom in my life which I did not really need at this time well what can I say.

I had my own place and now have a roommate to keep me busy and attending the church as a good servant but not yet a member just making myself useful and use my gifts and talents. But whenever my brother went out, we wanted to go with him, my roommate and I unless he took his wife out sometimes to socialize and meet other people because I was still fresh and new excited and anxious. There were times I would babysit and that worked out well, for a while until we wanted to go out more on the weekends, but did not know where to go, until my cousins would come and take me and my roommate out to be adventurous in this new State, this Big Beautiful City of my Dream.

It was one evening I believe and a few of us beautiful girls were going out on an adventure, or just going to show me in Los Angeles. We went to a nice hot spot in L.A. and began to frequent the town on the weekend with our short mini shorts and high heels, looking good of course on the where the nice sailor young men frequent. Which we continue for a year or more.

Well, in 1970 I met another nice young handsome navy man at a house party, in fact, a neighbor in the area. We began to date for one month or more, well we dated long enough to be comfortable and acquainted with each other for him to pop the question to me, very anxious to be married for all the wrong reasons, because I was selfishly, drawn to him, because he was in the navy with not previous spouse, and no children my mind was traveling, house, car, no responsibilities all about me. I shared it with my roommate and talked it over, so she would stay in the apartment as we searched for a house.

So, it happened. He was bold enough to buy me a ring beautiful rock, of course, my style and my choice. I'll tell you later.

He said, "WILL YOU" .......... and I spoke. "YES, I WILL" ...... But GOD did not say anything, Because I did not consult for His advice concerning this marriage. Gwen felt this was the one because he came with no agenda, so I thought, but everything I dreamed. Also, he was a navy man with what Gwen desired.

The lust of the eyes seemed so lovely and romantic at the time. I felt the urge and really thought It was time and I was ready to be married, so I decided to go for it, and just get married. He was nice and independent, single never been married, So I would be receiving those spousal benefits, (yes thinking all the wrong selfish thoughts, mind you), never met his parents, but his brother who was such a nice gentleman. I really believe Mr. M; B. was in love with me, and I was in love with the fringe benefits from his check and other extra privileges as his wife.

Well, God knew he came with baggage, (an agenda) but, I did not know his military mentality struck, whatever they call it but not a sickness or illness just narcissism and a Momma's boy although' I never met his parents, but I recognized the personality, which came along with him. We had just been acquainted a few months and he was about to return to the waters, on the ship, I wanted to get married to be his spouse to receive spousal military pay and he was ready to marry me because leaving me alone at home with my girlfriend was dangerous and he did not trust it, although it really did not cross my mind. We decided to get married before he had to leave for Port, which was a month in advance, notice and it is a good thing at the time to   for a while. Then when he returns, we would look for a house.

It all seemed so well, we started to buy a home, but I decided for him to move in with me my roommate and me until he returned from the Waters, it was a nice Apt. in Harbor City, and for now will do until he returns. I was moving fast, to become Mrs. Brown, and called my daddy to come out and do it right, well someone's parents had to be present, so why not my daddy meet this man, who would be marrying his daughter, then he would see what type of man he was, not that daddy was interested. So yes, my daddy had to come out for my first marriage to give me away. So, we moved into our nice little apt. close to my brother, (my suggestion) until he returns from Sea, then we would look for a house and let my roommate have the apartment. (that was the plan) I did not want to move too far from my brother, of course, he was the closest immediate family near me, and I was not moving too far from him. That was my instinct, rather than my spirit. So, I wanted to do this thing right, with my spiritual upbringing my daddy, Deacon Ralph Corbitt came out to give me away yes, indeed, he came out to give me away, and his brother (Mr. JJ, B ) was his best man, and my sister in law was my brides maid, my girlfriend was my maid of honor. Nice small family ceremony. Now he and his brother were like night and day, his brother was a nice young man.

So, here we are at my church I attended but never became a member. We had a nice humble sweet, ceremony in the church, it was just a tradition to be married in the church and the Pastor of the church was excited about the ceremony, where I attended and played the Piano, he probably anticipated us becoming members, but that was not on the horizon nor my radar.

It was just family and some friends I met in the Complex, and at work attended a little reception at our apartment a nice quiet reception, well not really, we partied most of the night. It all started out lovingly until my independence began to kick in during his time at sea and I wanted to have my way and continue to party. Of course, after my daddy returned home safely.

That did not last too long. Upon his return from the Waters, we began to search for a house in the neighborhood, nice brick and mortar, clay houses found and a nice house I liked but he did not like, it because it was too close to my brother. Well, I was not moving far from my brother who was out of the picture and his personality changed became an angry jealous, spoiled young man, and I became a selfish, spoiled independent angry BLACK woman again. Of course, all of this was after daddy arrived safely back home in New Jersey. Because my husband and my brother were not getting along at this time the blood was thicker than water. And my brother was not going to allow this man to continue in his actions. It was called the Military Syndrome of being on the water too long. I had no thoughts of moving away from my family. He began to dislike him, although they both served in the Navy but on different ships. In my endeavor to be the wife he desired, and I was close to my brother and family, there was dissention and they had words which began his military actions a became violent and Gwen is a fighter and will not back down.

Well, I did not want a divorce, just yet, but after the violence and my brother became involved it was time that we ended this adventurous, fairytale wedding. The marriage was on the rocks and my brother had to step in, so this was not looking good at all, and my girlfriend was not going to allow him to do too much, but he became too violent, and belligerent. She was a fighter also. Free with his hands and vulgar with his mouth. It was time to

"HIT THE ROAD JACK AND DON'T COME BACK NO MORE"

You ask me how long it lasted? I'll tell you how short it lasts. Well, we decided to get an annulment in six (6) months, yes indeed that's what I said six (6) months, it was over after he returned from ship duty. I was done with the marriage thing. It was not a good peaceful divorce. After the court case, he continued to apologize. My Attorney told me to give him everything he bought; of course, what women want to give up her beautiful furniture and appliances, But I realized my life and my family and friends meant more than materialist things and it was not the Lord's Perfect will and saying yes it was me and my flesh speaking out of greed. Because God knew what was best for me and it was not marriage at this time. I wanted a man with money, to buy me everything I desired, and yes, but as I said, baggage came, and I would pay the consequences again I did not know God's Perfect will and Permissive will for my life. Many times, we are walking in His Permissive will, not his Perfect will. He will speak and the answer is "NO," and we think He said "GO" but I felt in my spirit he told me to wait. but I just could not wait, this man wanted a sanctified woman, and I wanted a sanctified marriage, with all the trimmings, but couldn't wait on the Lord, walk by faith and be sanctified himself.

*"The bible says, "what God has joined together let no man put asunder" Matthew 19:6 (separate).... Well GOD did not join this union together, and I put it asunder, separate.*

Sometimes we become so anxious in our flesh and think of its love when it's a fairytale, or infatuation and realize it later after it's too late. We were marrying for all the wrong reasons. I wanted him to take care of me, and lavish clothing, big house, big car, supply my lavish needs and my fleshy needs, supply my financial needs money. And he promised to do all these things and I was ready for it all.

You see previously before my girlfriend came out to visit me I had met a girlfriend who was a military wife, and every time her husband went out to port, sea, she received and check until he returned and we would party until he returned Yes, it looked good sound good so this was easy and Mr. MB walked into my life, but, it just did not work out the way I planned it was not the Perfect will of God for my life. Where did I get this spirit from because it surely did not come from my parents, it came directly from my flesh, rushing marriage to have things, stuff, baggage, and sex. For all the wrong reasons, and not meeting anyone other than Mr. M.B. in the first stage of my adventure, and I was still carrying the hurt, of the promise, from my high school sweetheart. So, I will continue to "Adventure Land" of Los Angeles, Calif. That was the end of that.

Adventurous Fairy Tale Story Marriage. He was not me.

"SHINING ARMOR" on a WHITE STALLION"

# Chapter Nine
# The Departure of my roommate

*"There is a time for everything and a season for every activity under the heavens." Ecclesiastes 3:1*

We need to trust that God will always allow the right person in our life at the right time and for the right seasons. But we also must be willing to let the wrong people walk away. People come into our lives for a reason and a season but it's up to us to learn in that season, the message God is teaching.

Years passed, I reunited with my cousins, and we became, or should I say, a little more mature.

I will never forget my cousin taking me to different night clubs and hotspots, every weekend to familiarize myself with my Dream city just like a new kid on the block, I even had an opportunity to see where the Big Entertainers and Movie Star partied, and "Play boy Club", which you had to have a Key, of course, one of my Cousin worked for a big Corporation Co. and top of the penthouse with the revolving floor. This was all so new and exciting to me. But we only attended a few times on the weekend.

Then I was introduced to other nice nightclubs, where you had to come dressed in classy evening wear, not long gowns. because my cousins knew nice places in Los Angeles, and Hollywood. It was not as though' you saw a person in a movie on every corner, just a few throughout that area of Hollywood and even North Los Angeles which was close to Beverly Hills, this lasted until I received better employment and the partying ceased for a moment.

Well, my Roommate was leaving me because she had gotten home sick and all the excitement was a little too much, so she wanted to return back home to Pleasantville, New Jersey, I really did not blame her, because all her family was at home, but it was great company and visit with her, she enjoys her stay, but it was time for departure, and she will truly be missed by me in this apartment alone. But We had some great times together and it was such a joy to have her company, Although I did not mind being alone when you are comfortable with someone you know, you just don't want them to leave., But it's a Season for everything.

Now as she returned home, back to New Jersey, it was time for me to find a Real decent occupation to keep my head above water- because the vacation money was about to get really low, but always found time on the weekends to spend money and time together after all, we were finding ourselves in a new family relationship. There was so much I wanted to see and experience, not realizing there was more time than money. So, I began to quickly look for a Job, but it did not work out the way I planned, by this time I had a car note and rent to pay, with no husband or man on the horizon. The seed was planted in me and made me feel uncomfortable in my flesh, knowing the Holy Spirit was prompting the inner man instructing and preparing me for what was to come.

Sometimes you know what to do that is right and know what not to do which is the opposite. So, each week my cousin found something new for me to see do, and experience such as Universal Studios, Disney Land, go to San Diego for the San Diego Sea World and Zoo of course everyone wanted to visit here especially where some of the movies were established and how they were made in the Studios.

Initially, the first time it was overly exciting, then my other family and friends, after a few visits it became boring, and very repetitious, after viewing and seeing everything over, and over again. Because everyone who came to visit wanted to go to either Disneyland or Universal Studios sometimes both.

Until My Momma decided to make a visit and this time, I drove to Disneyland just learning how to drive on the freeway, so I thought I was driving well, until the Highway Patrol pulled me over for driving too slowly, on the freeway. That was a laugh for us, well, you know what took place. Afterwards, I learned how to drive like a native of California staying with the traffic, and it was not too slow.

But the outings of these Adventures kept me on the right road toward my change or transformation for a while, you know how you do little kidding stuff, you've never done before and you just want to do or continue to do them over and over as if someone was pushing you in a swing and you want to go higher and higher for fun, well this adventure was one alone with experiencing other beaches, in other Cities and Walks, there was an amusement park called "the pike" in Long Beach, California, similar to the boardwalk in Atlantic City, New Jersey but no boardwalks, just amusement rides and different fun activities, just walk along the beach. We stayed until the children got tired of the rides, games and eating popcorn, and ice cream, you know how the kids and adults enjoy outings.

Well, momma was leaving now until the next time. So, we had to get home early to help pack her bags, and make sure everything she bought would fit.

# Chapter Ten
# Home Sick

*"Cast all your anxiety on him because he cares for you."*
1 Peter 5:7

By now, I was getting home sick, my girlfriend returned home, and mom was safely home. I finally found a Job although' my cousins all had federal Government jobs. Now I wanted to see my New Jersey family, but just got this little job and could not leave right away. Yes, home sick, so now it was time for me to get settle in and get used to things. But I was becoming a little lonely for another family, My Momma and Daddy. I never spent too much time or was so far away from them this long. So, I had a TWA FREQUENT FLYER, then, of course, had a little job and could afford to travel back home every year for a while from 1968-69 it was SUMMER VACATIONS, time everyone was out ready for vacation. Janice, my cousin would go to Jamaica for vacation, with her friends from work and was not ready for that different vacation. So, I would go home to New Jersey, for a mini vacation. This made it so delightful for me, to travel home whenever I felt the need and felt lonely. That made me feel so Good to be able to travel home every year (thanks to TWA frequent flyer at that time) But it became expensive. I had to find another vacation spot close to home and get a decent job.

I wasn't ready to travel to the Bahamas or Jamaica as the others. So, by that time when I arrived back in Los Angeles from home, I made more friends, and we began to hang out and experience different adventures.

But, after visiting home, I really began to get lonely now for church and singing in the Choir all the Churchy stuff, because I have not been in a church setting, such as back at my home church in New Jersey. so, I began visiting again some of the many mega churches, I had seen on TV but, did not feel comfortable in my skin to become a member, there was much preaching and little fellowship, for sure as I entered the sanctuary it was that feeling just jumped on me, "oh how I miss church". Well, that did not last long, only on Sunday when someone invited me, but I was not ready to commit to anything at that time.

I bought a better car for traveling so it became quite expensive because I had no furniture due to my divorce or annulment. When it was settled, I gave it all back to Mr. MB, I did not want any strings attached and no spirits. So, I had to start over again. My cousin moved into her beautiful furnished Condo, we were forced to separate due to our jobs and the distance apart.

Well, you see by this time both of my brothers were discharged from the Military, and my oldest brother, James returned home to New Jersey Of course, Now I am almost on my own but desired to stay in California, my late brother Ralph Jr. stayed in California for a bit longer before moving to Tennessee after his discharge from Service.

We all went our separate ways. But continued to reside in California just a little while longer. Here I am in California a Single young lady, and that spirit of loneliness and anxiety tried to move in my life and spirit and not waiting on the Lord to bring me someone (man), I began to look, search for a mate to live with not to marry. Because that's the life I now live in the (flesh) even though the first one didn't work, I continued to obey the flesh and not the spirit.

So, a few years, later, I began to get comfortable in my own flesh, meeting new people and dating different men searching to see which one fit my lifestyle and my new place with their money, of course, it was just companionship and great company every now and then according to my agenda. You see at this time you had to dance to my music because it was either all of me or none. (Oops did I say that?)

So I started this new Job in Lomita California near the Harbor, thinking it was more money, Nursing Home (Residential Home) as a Nursing Assistant, learning all there was to learn about Nursing, it was very knowledgeable which was so amazing, this was my field, and vision before leaving home, did not know the Lord would lead me to the field of Nursing, or assisting, helping others, was my dream and further on to become an R.N maybe Nurse

Practitioner. But not yet, just for now, I am trying to settle down in my condo, new job and learning new people, and having much fun as a single lady touring all of Los Angeles Calif. Finally, another apt. in upper Los Angeles became too much for me commuting from west LA and working down in Lomita, Calif. Near the Harbor of course the freeways made the travel easier but a little bit faster and you had to get on at a certain time to beat the traffic. I found a better job in Torrance Cal. through one of the Registered Nurses since my desire was to pursue my nursing career. She informed me of one of the biggest hospitals in Southern California where I would be trained and certified.

HARBOR GENERAL HOSPITAL, which later became HARBOR UCLA MEDICAL CENTER, where at the time, trained as a Nurse Assistant, and receive a Certificate, again, but this was very intense training, at this time we assisted the Doctors and Registered Nurses, even administered medicine with assistance at times. Although I graduated from Manhattan Medical Assistant School in 1965 and received a Nursing Assistant Certificate of Completion from MMAS in Manhattan New York City, before coming to California, it was not accepted at Harbor UCLA Medical Hospital. So, we were trained and worked with a Harbor Certificate of Completion and on our way to work as a Nursing Assistant, called a Practical Nurse without a license, at that time this was quite an experience much different than the nursing home.

And began to meet interesting people of higher caliber in the field of Medicine, getting very acquainted with quite a few nice strangers, who became friendly, even though the Doctors and Registered Nurses were genuine with their knowledge. I even met some of my neighbors who were employed here at this hospital. It became quite an interesting Hospital to be employed. However, I became involved in the activities of others and began a different lifestyle out of the ordinary past.

As I began to receive experience, this prompted me to pursue my nursing career. There was a school I would enroll in called Southwest College, "Twilight Registered Nursing Program", in South Central Los Angeles, I would attend at night and earn my degree, but there was no opening for me to register at the time, so I kept it on my agenda in waiting for the next time enrollment open. Sometimes we can allow the enemy to smooth his way back into our lives unaware, waving nonsense in your face. During my waiting period, there were outside activities I loosely participated in.

Here in this town, so many people were coming into my space, of course, I allowed it, but they were so friendly, nice people mixed with ugly personalities and not-so-good activities. So, I used my discernment of those who were real and fake at this time. I decided to experience with some new acquainted associates and that was not a good idea at all. Well, yes, here, I met another young man and another young man, it appears these men were flourishing in my life for some reason, but none would I tell my momma about they were just acquaintances. They had an agenda lower than my plans, and God also had a plan, and I do not believe it was this plan.

*"For I know the plans I have for you,' declares the Lord, 'plans to prosper you and not to harm you, plans to give you hope and a future." Jeremiah 29:11.*

# Chapter Eleven
## Looking and finding Love in all the wrong places

*What is Love?*

*Love is patient and kind; love does not envy or boast.*
*It is not arrogant or rude.*

*It does not insist on its own way; it is not irritable or resentful.*
*it does not rejoice at wrongdoing but rejoices with the truth.*
*1 Corinthians 13:4–8a (ESV)*

LOVE IN ACTION
Transforming center says of MLK: Love in action is doing the
right thing, at the right time, in the right Spirit, completely given
over to a Power that is beyond our own– even, and perhaps most
especially, when the risks are very great.
"Every genuine expression of love grows out of a consistent and
total surrender to God."

Martin Luther King Jr.

Later my Big brother and his family decided they needed a change,
they too came out to move in with me also, for a change from
Pleasantville. We all lived together in this 3-bedroom big studio
apartment which wasn't so bad, but since they had two boys who
needed space, I decided to let them have the Studio apt. with 3
bedrooms, which was more room for them and I moved into my own

little condo, welcoming them with open arms, it was so good to see family come together, my cousins live in Los Angeles, not too far, and my other brother Ralph Jr. move his family to Tennessee.

So, my sister-in-law was blessed to find a position, at the same hospital, Harbor UCLA also. Shortly after my brother found a decent job.

Although my sister-in-law and I worked at the same hospital it was a huge hospital and they were still building, we had an old barrack campus, that was used for the army base, transformed into a hospital residence to camp out at night in case of emergencies. So, we did not see each other too often, she worked on different floors and at different hours.

Since my brother and sister-in-law were close, I had the opportunity to watch my two nephews grow up in the same area (Compton), graduate from high school then college and start their families. We socialize quite frequently with each other, especially on weekends, and holidays due to our working hours and had picnics, even our cousins had an opportunity to visit just fun, fun in the California Sun. We even went to some plays and shows, in the Hollywood area. Always found time for family gatherings on the weekends.

While I was having fun I met another nice sailor guy left over from my brother Ralph's friend just someone to kick it with, past time and then oops for a moment, but kept my apartment because he was (ship port duties) meaning out on the ship too much and too long and that was a bit too much for me in my single age and he was much older. So, I had to say goodbye quickly and, in a hurry, didn't want to break his heart. I believe he was looking for love and marriage, and he was not the one. So, I just kept it moving and the Lord was keeping me.

# PART THREE
## Chapter Twelve
## The Move

*"Woe to those who call evil good and good devil who put darkness for light and light for darkness who put bitter for sweet and sweet for bitter." Isaiah 5:20*

Well, now that I am on my own, learning by myself, trying to live on my own for the first time searching for a decent apartment, with a decent price, I found a small little cottage apt in South Central Los Angeles, better known as Compton, Calif. The city I heard of but had never interested me in living there, now was my opportunity to see and experience what I heard.

There was much moving for me in my dream state, trying to find myself.

But I was so proud of myself, my new home, apartment, and a new job, making my own money again, my single cousin and I continued to hang out and party the weekend. It is so different, because I never left home to live alone, especially in my own place. So finally trying to settle down here in Los Angeles and wanted to adventure, and experience everything. It was a hard decision for me. But somehow as I began to settle in my place choosing furniture, which was a fun thing to do for the first time with my cousin's help of course made the transition go smooth since they were familiar and I had no idea of where to start or what I really wanted, and how much it would cost me with all the furniture stores and there were plenty they were even selling brand new furniture on the corner streets, this is California and Compton, California from a warehouse and I mean real brand new furniture, but for my first time of course I want to buy out of the familiar store.

So that was completed in 2 days, Now I am ready to be the host of most. Ready to entertain the company by meeting more new people. but as I prepared myself to entertain, I received a call from another school mate desired to come out to be my roommate so worked out and planned in the nick of time. It was great company for me for a short time.

I had not attended Church in a while since receiving my new job and my own new place, because it was not on my agenda or Radar as we say. since I left Harbor City, my brother Ralph's area. I thought it was time now to find a church nearby and try to settle down to please my mom, (here I go again trying to please the wrong person) not knowing this was for me and my life. But I did not begin right away, Gwen continued to do what she desired in her flesh, and I know God was not pleased with the life I began to live, but He loved me so much that he kept his hands on me, and a fence around me. And it was all for His plans no one knew His business like He did.

I began to date different men and they would introduce me to the night scene, wine and dine me, with dancing all night sometimes I stayed out until daybreak and came home to sleep all day, of course, this was the weekend so there was no going to church in the horizon, and this was certainly not Gods plan.

We would meet at lunch and after work to continue our activities. I kept going out with my girls (employees) from the hospital enjoying having fun, good time, and meeting other nice men, they would wine and dine me and then offer to take me home but no sir, my girls would take me home. Then I began to meet some of my brother's sailors, tall, very handsome men. Well, we dated for a month, then I met a real man, and dated for months, but no marriage was insight or on the horizon for me, not yet I just wanted to have fun and enjoy myself. Then the enemy stepped in and introduced me to marijuana, on a high note, then Cocaine, and began to go down the road of disaster and destruction, being distracted by the enemy, I began to sleep with the enemy, he supplied my fleshy desires. I had no knowledge of what was going on in my life, because I looked at it as fun, calling evil good, and good evil never as distraction or destruction, gradually moving into darkness, but it was looking as though' it was light, and my sweetness began to change to bitterness, became a functional user, though, I kept my hospital job because I knew how to pretend and talk my way in and out. Always looking the best clean and dressing the best. I met my drug dealer, real smooth, quiet, and sweet, who worked at the hospital also. Whatever I needed or wanted from him he supplied. He was such a nice guy to me, but I know he was not my "knight in shining armor" we would take vacations together, as we made drop-offs in different places. although' I had my apt., and he had his own palace. We just had fun together as we called it at that time. two mature adults in the night light. Until I found out he was married, well did that have influence? NO. Really nothing made a difference in my life but living my life as I pleased when I pleased, and how I pleased.

> Woe to those who call evil good and good evil,
> who put darkness for light and light for darkness,
> who put bitter for sweet?
> and sweet for bitter."

So here my life was spiraling downward when it was supposed to move forward toward betterment, and changing before my eyes and I did not recognize, due to influential male and female partners, who later became my BFF men of the night and day. The girls or ladies I met were my associates, and party BFF friends were women of the Ladies so that was my activities, although' we had good jobs, this was our lifestyle on the weekend. We got involved with what we called high rollers, handsome, military, and businessmen, and brought whatever we desired.

We met another young lady who had more knowledge concerning the business. She had a gated apartment building where the drugs flowed freely and had security. I continued to keep my job, and my money, learned how to function and continued with my habit, I found a gated apartment near my supplier, He had a white Saint Bernard Dog, not dangerous just looked the part, but he was a playful puppy. People did not know he was not dangerous; his bark was bigger than his bite. When we stepped out, we never appeared to look as though' my activities controlled us.

Always dressed well, kept myself smelling good and looked clean, every time I went to work. No one ever knew what activities I was involved in at the time but my close girls. Just to be open we were very classy, dressed well, working ladies, good Jobs, always kept money. This is what you call a FCA "Functional Classy Addict."

I want to be incredibly open and transparent in my testimony, my activities, and how God kept me for His plan, as He received the Glory from my life, as He gave me His Grace and Favor, every day which I did not deserve. You may witness this or share the same testimonies.

However, there were consequences. As I continued with this lifestyle for a while, with my male friends and others, there was no time for church or church activities. (Putting my religion on the back burner until later) Sunday began to be my rest and fun day, inner action day or my sleep-in, resting day. After sleeping late, we would meet at our friends at a gated, luxury Condo, for Bar B Q parties, live music and trimmings, a swimming pool, jacuzzi, and sauna you had to have a key to enter because she was a tax consultant by trade, and a house woman (madam) interest, however, she handled, and maneuver was her business. So, we frequent often for benefits such as receiving a great return every year on my taxes, allowing her to maneuver, using fictitious names, and social security yes, I said there were consequences, later down the road, by paying back later but it was a joy while it lasted.

Well as the story goes, my male friend and I decided after a few years it was time we had our own business, at that's what I thought for a few years as a "High Ping dealer," until one evening, attending a classy party and not knowing a bad deal was in the house and there was some disruption, shooting and missing me and my male friend, by the Mercy and Grace of God. Now that was a warning for me in the wrong place and the wrong time, entertaining the enemy in the enemy's camp. This was our last time in that house and a warning for me to get myself and my life together and end this fantasy relationship and business while I still have this life that belongs to the Lord. But did I listen to the spirit speaking to me? Well, I was still walking in the flesh and not the spirit of Christ, because there was no unction in my flesh, my mind was on looking for love to enjoy and entertain in my new Condo. Well, my male friend would stay overnight we had our own party and one thing led to another he indulged in too many alcoholic beverages and narcotics. we fell in love for a moment maybe a few years, we anticipated marriage, but it was not going to work, because we were both in the wrong business, with two different mindsets I knew what was in my spirit and this was not love for me, just another convenient fantasy.

He looked good, he did good, he made me feel good, all the time, and at the time, it was good. But there was something that just did not feel good on the inside.

I was looking for LOVE IN ALL THE wrong places and in love with the wrong things and wrong people.

# Chapter Thirteen
# New Atmosphere

*Many plans are in a person's heart, but the LORD's decree will prevail.*
*(Christian Standard Version) Proverbs 19:21*

*Many plans are in a man's mind, but it is the LORD's purpose for him that will stand (be carried out)*
*Proverbs 19:21 (Amplified version)*

*We humans keep brainstorming options and plans, but God's purpose prevails.*
*Proverbs 19:21 (The message Bible)*

# "enjoying life with a new experience"

I can remember so well my time in my nice place enjoying my new apartment in Compton, Calif. New Atmosphere. I loved my little home upstairs, with 1 bedroom and a small balcony.

But I did not acknowledge God in my life, and I had one of the biggest scares on my health I never want to experience again. So, as I continued to chase man (following my flesh) and not God, enjoying bright lights in the big city, I became very painfully, critically sick in my new apartment, until I had to call my big brother, James. Thank God He didn't live far from me. Well, he had to pick me up as though' he was picking up a baby in his arms literally carry me to his car, and take me to the emergency Kaiser hospital in Harbor City, although' I worked at a Hospital but this Hospital which was not far, just around the corner but it seemly was a long distance because every bump on the road was felt and I really thought it was damaging my insides. When I arrived at the Harbor City Kaiser Permanente Hospital, they looked at me of course they had to examine me but when they touched my abdomen with their finger, I gave out a yell, I mean a scream they took me right to surgery, I had a ruptured appendicitis, and umbilical hernia and stomach ulcer. Well, had I laid in my bed any longer, I would not have made it through the night, my brother would have found his sister dead in her apartment. IT WAS Only the Goodness and the Mercies of God that kept me.

I stayed in the hospital for a month or more seemingly a year. When I was discharged, my sweet mother flew out from New Jersey, this time to nurse me back to health. We went to get her from the Airport, she was happier to see me than I was to see her, because of what I had just experienced and continue to be healing and recovering, moving very slowly. So, my mother dearest, stayed for a couple of weeks or more until I was able to go back to work, at my brother Ralph Jr. since He had a larger house. I believe she experienced an earthquake during her stay. She didn't know what was happening at the time, just felt a shaking, then we revealed to her it was an earthquake. Afterward of course we then had to take her to the beach, the Pacific Ocean. Unbelievably to mix some of the Pacific Ocean in a jar to take home with her, and mix with the Atlantic Ocean, at time you were able to carry anything on the plane with no fee. Then of course we had to visit Disney land, (not Disney world) and others.

Amusement parks with Grandmom and her Grandchildren before heading back to New Jersey. We went to visit her nephew and Nieces (her deceased sister's children) We had a great family reunion unplanned, but they are the best kind.

Well, it was time for my mama to return home, sadly, I really did not want her to leave, but my daddy needed her back home. She was the best nurse, ever, well she was momma, the one who gave birth to me. I was not fully recovered but ready to return to work. So of course, the first thing I will do is search for a church near my home, apt. around Compton area just to please my parents, and really please my heavenly Father who kept me, and healed me, I had that much maturity to realize something was missing in my life, and it was time for me prepare for the change and begin to seek it. I know my parents would be happy and not worry about my safety and Christian life.

Something was pulling me in to begin a turn around. I was there in my change of life for the better, feeling it all inside, did not know what was taking place but I know it was a different feeling, it you can call it a feeling. Never like this before, but my flesh was pulling away from, and my spirit was moving forward. I did not understand what was going on, and became nervous, anxious and all my emotions were confused. But I did not let this pull me backwards, because I met some sisters, at that time, who knew the Lord, and encouraged me, that knew what was going on, and continued to reach out to me and stay in touch. God was moving through them to me. I was enjoying life, but God wants me to enjoy the Abundant Life.

# Chapter Fourteen
# From Preparation
# Comes
# Transformation

*"Do not be conformed to this world, but be TRANSFORMED by the renewing of your minds, so that you may discern what is the will of God—what is good, acceptable, and perfect."*
Romans 12:2-3

I began to show signs or act as if a changed life was being activated looking the part but oh what a change in my life or it was in progress, well, you would think after my trauma, miracle, and almost death experience, I would take heed of the warning signs. And now that my mom has returned home, it was time for me to bring it all together so she would not have to worry about her big girl. God has spared my life once again, but how soon did I forget it? Well, as soon as my mom returned back to Pleasantville, NJ, and I knew she was safe at home, the Lord had healed my body and I was back to enjoy my life in California, just loving it and doing what I desired after all, this was my dream state and on my bucket list.

This time the Lord led me to a good group well a little Religious Sunday afternoon activity. I met some people in a park who asked me to join them in a choir, so I decided to at least give it a try, but it did not work out for me at this time, my mind was not clear, and my heart was not in the right place, so I continued to visit other sanctuaries West Angeles, COGIC, the late James Cleveland, and others, where I would sit in church and enjoy real church, real singing real worship real music, and a Powerful, Anointed Word from the Lord of course all my BFF were transformed renewed and working. I was enjoying the gospel singing all over Los Angeles California. Really, I was Church hoping Around town, not desiring to join any church at the time.

The well-known professional singers or preachers would show up on a Sunday Morning or afternoon Service, at a big, huge theater church in the heart of L. A. called 54th and Central Church in South Central Los Angeles. You will hear me speak of this church throughout this part of the book. It was a hot spot-on Sunday, this is where you see all the famous singers, even movie stars as ordinary people.

So, I began to travel alone, in my Sunday Best dress with my Sunday suit and hat, yes, they were wearing hats then most of the time. When it was time for me to leave church there was no one to hinder me, no one obligated me from my time. But after church, I would still visit one of my cousins who did not work on Sunday, which   to me, no work on Sundays, it was religious purpose, if I decided to become a member, my Sunday would always be available. Somehow, my cousin and I would always make arrangements to either go out of town or just hang at the beach, during day, and club at night, because the weather was so beautiful to just stay in the house, come home early to prepare for work, but we did it purposely to stay in good health and not be tired the next day at work. That was our routine schedule for a moment until she moved to North Hollywood in a nice quiet, beautiful club house Condo. This was too far at times for me to travel alone, but we managed to socialize at her Condo, and I would sleep over, and go to work from there taking that long drive from North Hollywood to Torrance California on the worst, freeways, in the morning, 101 and 405 so that did not last long.

I finally recuperated from my surgery, which forced me to slow down and use wisdom and common sense. Since my brother James and his wife and family were still living here I decided to visit them more often on Sunday to stay out of trouble, but that did not last for a very long time, you see being free and I mean real free, your own apartment/condo and car coming and going when at any time no curfew, that was freedom to me. So, I met a friend of a friend, and we began to date. Now this was a religious guy who frequents the church every now and then, so I thought this was the opportune time to visit church with him. I believe he sang with a quartet, no name, it appeared at our favorite place on 54$^{th}$ street and Central Ave. in South Central Los Angeles, at an Old Huge Movie Theater, Church Building, where they would had different Concerts every Sunday, Sponsored by James Cleveland and Los Angeles Choir of course many other choirs, and spiritual groups as I mentioned, this was a hot fired place to go on Sunday afternoon if you really wanted to hear some Great Powerful Singers.

So, I followed him for a few Sundays and met some other people, young ladies who invited me to another Concert which was in downtown Los Angeles. In trying to find my purpose or my interest in singing or church, I was led to another singing group, by a religious cousin on the other side of town (I was not interested in confining myself to a particular group or church) called the "ANOINTED ONES" although I began to get excited and involved with this singing group and traveling with them throughout the city. Enjoying different singing groups around Los Angeles City. We would attend the programs for free, but this lasted for a few years until I met some other young ladies. I was still in the flesh, but the spirit of singing was instilled in me, and I just could not let it go.

Although' I was learning my Dream State, and enjoying the journey, it was clean, positive activities, in this beautiful City of

Angeles, with beautiful weather, just how I dreamed it to be and love, love, love it, everything appeared to be the right place at the right time. I was so excited, but I was still working at the hospital, so I went to bed early.

Well, they invited me to another Concert in the downtown area of Los Angles again where I've never been, but I was like a kid with an Ice Cream Cone we all got together and traveled with them. We began to speak of our future and our mission and musical desires to become a participant of one of these choirs, which required audition and time. So, we inquired about the rehearsals or choir,

so before I knew it, I joined another choir called. **"THE WATTS COMMUNITY CHOIR"** Now in this phase of my life I began to look at life a little differently and the seed that was planted in me by my parents began to rise, grow, and mature a bit. Well, this time something inside began to awaken and stir up the gift of God's birth inside me, which was my singing something I enjoyed, and the seed Mom and Dad planted in my spirit. At this time, we were not mature enough to participate in this Concert.

We arrived, at the concert it was one of the largest Auditoriums in downtown Los Angelos, called the "Embassy Auditorium," where all the largest Gospel Artists held Concerts. As I sat there on the balcony listening to all the different choirs from all over Southern and Northern, California area, I had no idea they were famous choirs, such a Los Angeles, Mass Choir, James Cleveland singers, Walter Hawkins, his brother, and Love Center Church, from Northern California, others there were so many from everywhere, and it was free will offering. I had never seen anything like this until I came to California. On the east Coast at different churches, we always had to invite singers from out of State if they were important or Professionals, or just the singing groups in the area would gather, but not in this upscale category. This was so exciting to me, and the Ladies were so cordial and humble.

Well, Mr. George Washington, Conedy happens to be the musician for many of them, if not all, in that category. Then they called this short, handsome, fair-skinned man with a long bushy natural hairstyle and clean-cut mustache, in a white suit and white shoes, to walk across the stage to accept a Music Trophy Award of the year. He was so humble as he received it. But I looked at him, our eyes met, and in my spirit that was going to be my "knight in shining Armor" His name was George Conedy, one of the greatest musicians in the Los Angeles Area. It was in my head the both of us doing Music Ministry together.

Well, after speaking to him and having conversations with him, we (I) developed a very friendly relationship but that was not on my mind and in my spirit, just being real Now, I was looking at more than a spiritual relationship. I believe that It was God's divine intervention for me to be in the right place at the right time but for HIS purpose, and plan, or just say it was God's timing and my intervention, but not he would be the one to introduce me to my new church, and Gods plan for him to lead me to a church and that was all nothing else but, He was going to do a new thing in me if I allowed him and I did allow him to do His finish work in my life develop a real relationship with him.

Months went by before I really met him personally. Then it was a few years later when we really hooked up, I had to make sure with the Lord he was the right one. But there were some other issues God had to work on in our lives. Because we both had to be delivered from drugs and alcoholic activities.

Somehow, we met later and Mr. George Conedy, led me to a church in Compton close to where I lived, Little Mount Zion Baptist Church, now better known as "The Greater Mount Zion where he was the musician. This was fantastic.

Well, George invited me to visit again and again. My spirit felt right, I felt at home and the need to make this my church home, but not so quickly, and become an official member after visiting so many other churches in Compton. So here I was at the Little Zion Missionary Baptist Church, under the late, Dr. Jerome Fisher Pastor, became my Pastor so now I could call my mother and inform her of this new church, and I became involved by this young man who played the Hell out of a Hammond B3 Organ, (of course, did not say it in that terminology) but the BEST MUSICIAN in the WEST and most popular Musician in the Los Angeles area.

Well, little did I know that he was married, with three (3) babies. Well, Lord now what? seemingly God was working things out for my good, so here we are meeting, and the organist for this Choir, "Watts Community Choir" my friends wanted me to stay in ok Lord what is happening now, He has (3) three babies not one (1) but three, and I quite sure he is still connected to his wife with all those babies and we were becoming intimate. (in fact, which was my vision and purpose, not God) Don't get me wrong they were beautiful girls, no boys. So now, all I want to do is hook up with him, use my gift and talent, sing, and find my way back in the church and have him accompany me, my thoughts and my vision are locked around Mr. Conedy as MY MUSICIAN.

So, I find the opportunity to sit down in my nice apartment and speak to him concerning this but not so well as we were about to mix business with pleasure, and this will not work out. Now, we have become good soft friends or acquaintances because we enjoyed each other's company. So, would you believe he invited me to the same choir in WATTS, CALIF? Led by his friend, the late "D.J. Rogers, "I became a member, and sang throughout L. A. County then we began to travel all over singing in Southern Calif. Las Vegas, other towns, and cities, under our Producer, (Bro. Henry) aka Mr. Henry, who had a radio broadcasting station. Later in the year the

**"Watts Community Choir** was well known and sang on many different Christian programs and TV networks to open shows and services for famous singers and church services. (Bro. Henry) aka Mr. Henry sponsored us in our first ABC TV show called "The Jimmy Durante Show" every time it aired, we received royalty checks and that was good money to me. George also had the opportunity to record one Christmas album of his own. (They were albums at the time.) 78's.

Although I was still working at the Hospital there was an opportunity for me to join the church choir, I Became one of the lead singers in the Mass choir and then director of the Senior Choir then organized the rosebud choir, between the ages of 3-8, they were a joy of my heart. The Lord began to show me my purpose, but was I ready? And prepared to step in it? NO!

Then later, I invited him over for Sunday Dinner, well would you believe, he would come with his own food a 6 pack of

Budweiser Beer and a box of "Churches chicken. This was the juices, greasy, black chicken you ate when you were hungry, but it was good "any how" this was his signature to have a conversation. It was alright with me because that was not my drink, with the exception when it was really hot, then I would drink it for a cooler that's all just a refresher, beer had no taste. Well, moving ahead.

Well, I thought I was falling in love of course began to date after rehearsal and even after church rehearsal this was not my "knight in shining armor" with Children. Someone introduced me to, but I was not ready to settle down with him. Although I enjoyed his music ministry a Maestro on the Organ. Very Popular throughout Los Angeles California in Great Demand for his outstanding Musical abilities and serious concerning his music ministry.

I received a call to join another choir, and this was my dream to be in a choir that sang on Sundays. Holding on to my job with every Sunday off was great, I believe this was the Lord's doing. But after being there for months people became jealous of my talent and gift in the group. Well, you know how that goes, they want you when if they can use you. So, my flesh goes in the way again, due to my anger.

I was introduced to drugs "marijuana, cocaine, and speed. this was my time for freedom to go and come, too much freedom began to sell drugs, not only that but steal them and sell on the streets.

Then I met a young man (high class drug dealer) and developed a relationship with him, and he became my drug dealer, but we were a highly sophisticated, secret drug, ring, that also involved Ministers and corporate people not allowed to mention names or churches.

Many people do not understand this, nor can they receive the fact that you can fall away, backslid when you are not in a spirit-filled serious group of people, even if the seed was planted in me to do work for the Lord, but I chose to do work on the side for myself.

This forced me to make a negative turn around, Now I have an excellent paying job. Trained as a nursing assistant with a certificate at this time working good hours, but returned to my bad habits, as Paul says In Scripture, *"when I desire to do good evil is always present"* I allow my flesh to dictate to me.

A few years later, my brother and his family decided to move to another location called Long Beach, leaving me in another part of California alone. I'm a big girl now, so I thought in my own eyes, on my own, in my Dream State of California. So, I had to put on my Big Girl Pants and Live on my own. Now here I was drifting backwards instead of moving forward in my music career for the Lord. During this time, I met many different people of all walks of life, who befriend me. God had HIS hands on me and a FENCE ALL AROUND ME.

# Chapter Fifteen
## THE PROCESS

*Behold, I will do a new thing, now it shall spring forth; shall ye not know it? I will even make a way in the wilderness and rivers in the desert.*
*(Isaiah 43:19)*

# We Need to Maximize Redemption and Minimize sin.

**Maximize:**

make it as large as possible.

**Redemption:**

The action of regaining or gaining possession of something in exchange for payment or clearing a debt; freeing from sin, repurchase, exchange, paying back, making good, being saved from sin "God's plan of Salvation."

**Minimize:**

Make it as small as possible.

**SIN:**

Make as none as possible.


At the end of the day, people won't remember what you said or did, they will remember how you made them feel.
Maya Angelou


People want to know how much we care, not how much we know, or how much knowledge acquired.
Unknown


It is not effective when we do not give of ourselves what the Holy Spirit imparts in us.
Unknown

# "Learning the Process"

Many times, I continue to walk in my own fleshy plans and not the plan of God isn't this what we do most of the time, ignoring our Christian upbringing, and his ways and later not understanding why He continued to take care of us even in our messy life, and really, I mean my messy life, but God is so faithful, in all His ways. I did not understand why situations occurred and I repeatedly continued to fall back into my sinful state. Sometimes it feels good to our flesh unknowingly but there were some consequences that went along with walking in the flesh.

You see my flesh was dominating, and desired things of my fleshly nature, but when trouble came and began to fall.

God was there to bring me back into the fold not knowing Mama and Daddy were praying for me. I had not developed an intimate relationship with the Lord Jesus, and this made my relationship with Christ all on the surface and not in the heart. It was an open door for the enemy to walk in and take over. Then on the other hand others would judge and define me, when in reality, no one understood what God was up to in my life. We are uniquely designed by God's hand, created as his masterpiece, exclusively for his work, and we are no accident, incident, mishap, or oops baby in his eyesight, we are HIS "MASTERPIECE" HIS "Piece of Work" allow me to minister just a few minutes please, before we move forward into being prepared for the journey, and if you are reading this now, remember, you are a spiritual treasure for Gods Glory."

Let me put it this way as Paul speaks in Ephesians 2:10 in the bible,

We are God's masterpiece, His handiwork, His workmanship. And then Peter says:

*"But you are chosen generation, a royal priesthood, a holy nation,*
*a peculiar people;" I Peter 2:9*

I just had to stop and submit this now. You are a mistake getting ready to happen, and you are not reading this just by happenstance, or you stumbled on this book. God has more work for you and wants to use you in His Kingdom to bring someone to Him whose heart is open and ready to receive him.

God never left me alone, and He kept his hand of love strength and power on me, just to let me know, "it's not by my power nor my strength but only His Spirit."

He will keep you that HE will receive Glory.

There's a song by the late James Cleveland that goes like this:

"OH, TO BE KEPT BY JESUS,

LORD AT THY FEET I FALL,

KEPT BY THE POWER OF GOD,

I WOULD BE NOTHING, NOTHING, NO NOTHING,

THY SHALL ALL AND ALL"

And as I come to the Preparation and Transformation although there is so much more, I experienced in the forty (40) years in California, as I write my story I am really reliving, praying, and thanking God for my life, as you notice scriptures from the bible are throughout my books, showing that something was alive inside me. It is the word of God that will continue to keep me. No one will understand and some will not believe, but yes this is all behind me and I thank God for the journey and the coming out. Now I can continue to tell the story of how my marriage, church family and immediate family were born and existed here in California. It really all started in Compton California after everyone left me there alone but overly excited in the process of preparation. Really God was preparing me for something I could not handle in the beginning.

# "Going through the Process"

So here I am in my preparation on the way to Transformation, in *the process* but unaware, that I was in the middle of it and how to maneuver through it.

Now I am in church not knowing God was building something inside me. In the last chapter I met the late George Conedy, (playing the Hammond B3 Organ) by this time I was introduced to Little Zion Baptist Church in Compton Calif. Where he was the organist. I finally became a member and began to get involved in the Choir (the voices of Zion) this was one of the greatest choirs in Compton, Calif. I was still participating in the Watts Community Choir, and church hoping to try to find the right church,

What was the right church for me?

How did I know what was right and what was wrong?

Who was I following at the time?

My flesh, the crowd, or the spirit?

Well, I did not have answers to these questions then, but I know now. OH, OH YES INDEED.

During this time as I began to attend the church in Compton, as George introduced me, and where he was the Organist, we became friends because of our music abilities, and I began to sing in the choir and enjoyed it so much, that I quit the other outside choirs and tried to settle down for once in my lifetime and prepare to see what God had for me to do in this church. So, when I finally settled in this church, I called mom and told her all about this church in Compton and all about the preacher.

Well, would you believe I became so involved in this church, I invited my brother and sister-in-law, and they became members, in fact they were involved in different ministries. I became one of the lead vocalists and enjoyed every moment of this, but still was not saved and filled with the Holy Ghost. I really want to take my time with this. I met the Pianist, the late Mattye White, we became buddies, she and her wonderful family, also the Minister of Music Bro F. W. and all the other musicians, a great group of people and musicians of course Mr. Conedy led the musicians.

I became familiar with most of the people it was a flourishing, growing, exciting, popular church in the City of Compton and the Pastor and choir were in demand to sing throughout Compton Los Angeles Calif. We began to travel in and out of different states because the pastor and choir were so in demand. We had an engagement every month if not every Sunday afternoon. Whenever we appeared at a church throughout Los Angeles County, the choir loft was too small, we were called (Pharaohs Army) by others. On holidays although the church was large, we had to rent a school auditorium to have service. There was a jr. High school adjacent to the church that we would rent every Easter, we looked forward to this every year, just to see the people crowd the auditorium and we march down the aisle with our beautiful robes and believe or not there were more people to attend than I had seen in years at other churches I attended. At the time my Daddy heard of him and wanted him to come to New Jersey, so it happened, my daddy made it happen, Pastor Jerome Fisher flew into Atlantic City, New Jersey and had a week's revival, my daddy was so excited, not sure but I think it was an annual thing for about 2 years maybe. My daddy even had James Cleveland there at one time, in Atlantic City.

There were so many young people attending and, becoming a member of this church, I had a desire to be a part of the young people's department to assist. Well, this began my preparation for purpose. There were so many young people in the Adult Choir that it was time to separate them from the Adults, of course with the Pastors' permission.

I formed a youth and young adult choir from most of the young people little did I know they were just as interested as I was in becoming their leader. I began to find interest in more of the young ladies than the young men, but some were troubled young people. So, as I began to take an interest in them, we became a Youth and Young Adult Department with many activities. Well, I needed a musician for the choir although I played a little bit, but not as great as Mr. Conedy, and other musicians in Cal. So, he became our musician as well as the church musician and this met, we had to rehearse together whether it be at the church or at his apartment, I did not want him to know where I lived at the time, but little did we know, this was God's plan for our future not how we orchestrated but it happened. We became close in church, and at home and began to date and the rest is history in the next chapter.

# Chapter Sixteen
## *The Wedding Vows*

WELL, IT HAPPENED. WE FELL IN LOVE and began to playhouse with not house rules and of course, after his divorce, a year later I oops had a baby out of wedlock and inherited 3 beautiful darling baby girls. Well, they were not really babies but, 3, 4, and 5 years of age. I was afraid to call my mother all the way in New Jersey to let her know, I guess it was respect for momma since I was working in church and doing so good, trying to be obedient in one way but, not in another way.

So, I called my sister in New Jersey and told her, and she told my mom, oh well. You see my sister was already really married and had a nice large wedding years before me, infect I was her maid of honor, but she had one (1) daughter we always talked about then. She did it the right way, (not her way) So, we (George and I) decided to get married and do it Gods way and our parents' way, because see George was raised as (COGIC) Church of God In Christ, His Mother, Father and entire family were saved, sanctified, and filled, My mother was ok with that until this. She loved him because he was a church boy, just as I was a church girl.

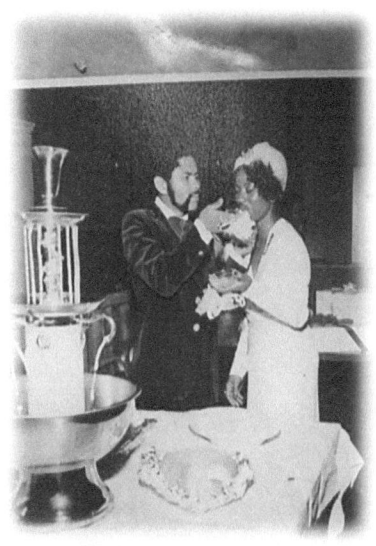

Well, we got married by the late Pastor Fisher, (who encouraged us to marry, and who was our Pastor at the time) in his new Home (Mansion) he and his wife had just purchased. My brother-in-law was his best man and my sister-in-law, was my Maid of honor.

George was a Union Musician in a professional band playing for weddings, conventions, and other big affairs a band connected with the city, called the "Magnetic Minds" etc. night club in throughout the Los Angeles area, whenever they called them, he had to be there. Since he was connected to the city, his manager allowed us to have our reception and the band played free, at one of the big dining halls, night clubs on Sunday, no charge.

It was such a grand occasion, all my family, his family friends and church members came after church, the musicians George was familiar with and their families. Since we did not have a big wedding, or an elaborate reception (and not so much money, which I desired) this was wonderful. At this time, we had our little 7-month-old fat baby boy, my bundle of joy, who slept throughout the entire reception going from arm to arm everyone wanted to love him and have more pictures of him as though' it was his birthday. I had my little George (baby George), and I was happy. Now I was on my way from Preparation moving into Transformation.

As God orchestrated his plan for my life. I did not know as I was leaning toward my understanding, but now acknowledging God's plan for my life.

*We can make plans, but the LORD's purpose will prevail. Proverbs 19:21 (NLT)*

When God has a plan for you it will come to pass for His purpose, and He will receive the Glory.

For I know the plans I have for you, "declares the LORD, plans to prosper you and not to harm you, plans to give you hope and a future." Jeremiah 29:11

I was afraid of what was next for my life, here is me, yesssss me with a baby and a husband (27) and I was 29 in the later stage of my life, at the age of that never knew about in my life, only watched mother at home, but now it's my chance to be a parent and a wife.

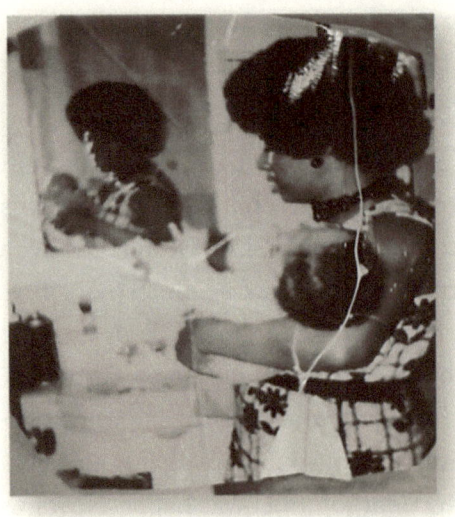

Well, I had the (3) girls most of the time, because that's the way he wanted them to be familiar with their new brother and stepmother. They were extremely helpful in caring for their brother, of course, he thought it was fun having them around, but he was so fat they could not hold him and play with him. My brother named him "meatball" and his sons began to call him "meat" as a nick name until he got married, they continued to call him that even though he slimmed down.

So here I am a married trying to be the best church Mother, a woman of God serving in the capacity of a ministry, and a wife and mother,  not knowing because of my smoking, during my pregnancy, which I did not know too much, My Son always kept a cold and shortness of breath, I stayed in Kaiser Permanente hospital, Emergency, I had no idea that my son what's suffering from chronic acute asthma until I went to the doctor, the second time and they noticed that was always staring emergency and so Crisis Respiratory clinic called me and told me to bring him in for testing and when I went into crisis clinic they scared so they examined him and gave him medicine because he was coming home from school every day I was running from work to school to get him to emergency. and so, this is when they diagnosed him with acute chronic asthmatic upper respiratory disease and you would have thought that my child had a few days to live and so this is what really prompted me to me from preparation to transformation because I had to make up my mind, about my life. At the time I was working in the hospital at the time I was working in harbor UCLA Medical Center at the time but I had no idea what to do with a baby with Respiratory disease and acute chronic asthma and this went on for years, since he was born in High School years, he had this acute he had this disease I call it a disease. I had called everybody who knew how to get a prayer to the throne room. the church from the West Coast to the East Coast I had everyone here in New Jersey praying and everyone I knew here, of course my in-laws were praying night and day, midnight hour.

The ladies who met me were praying for me, and God did a miracle. At one time I thought God was punishing me for my life, but it was my lifestyle, which caused him to initially have this disease. That's what really changed my heart and life, transformed my life sometimes God put things in your way to open your eyes to see the bigger picture, but I thank God at that time!!! YES, it was time for a change in my life. it was time, YES, it was time for my change it was time for me to be serious about God and develop a real relationship with Him. My son went through high school with this terrible disease which I had no idea of how to treat it and so instead of me asking for forgiveness I pray to God, and I asked him why my child you know we always want to know why our children or why me and then I had to look back over my life and realize. God was trying to get my attention to live for Him and not for myself.

Someone encouraged me with these words.

Sometimes life get hard,

Sometimes you don't know what to do.

But Remember at all times ....

God is with you; He will never leave you alone.

I thought that he was punishing me I thought God was punishing me through my child but it really was my it was filthy living as I wanted to live in sin, my smoking, and drinking, that triggered it my husband smoked and I smoked both drank alcohol, that's what triggered acute asthma asthmatic it was transferred from my body into my sons' lungs during my pregnancy and I there was a time I never thought that my child was going to live throughout the day, or night, he had to sleep with us because he had could not breathe at night, and I became afraid, fear had settled in my spirit because of had how I lived and took so long coming back to God. There were no treatments.

I feared for him to get up and take him to an emergency, repeatedly, running to the hospital so that they could give him treatment. There was no breathing machine at the time, in this Century. I Praise Almighty God for saving me, for keeping him, through my little faith and prayers and the prayers of the Saints of God, and church family, He was healed miraculously, learning how to take care of his body and understand his disease. Thank God that he was healed. God was watching over us, not for us but to let us know how much He cared and loved us. I believe Jesus had His hands on me from all the time, just to see if I was going to come in out of the storm or continue to stay in my destructive Sinful Nature. GOD HAD A PLAN.

Now, as choir director of the young adult choir, and my husband George Musician. That went along just nicely for years. We also traveled with his anointed family singing at concerts, and other churches, also participating in drama plays as he would travel as a musician on the road, and I would pack up the kids preparing to stay overnight. His Mother which we call (Mother Dear) because she was a mother Dear to everyone, and evangelized, full of the Holy Ghost, a strong, "CHURCH OF GOD IN CHRIST" woman of God. Most of our outings were without the kids.

We joined a Gospel group called the "AGAPE SINGERS" at Inglewood High School as a musician of the "AGAPE SINGERS, and through this, she organized a children's choir called the "Little Agape Angels" consisting of our children of the Singers of course we were one of the families. We began to travel with our children but that did not last too long.

You see my husband was very short-tempered and had a nervous problem and if it took too long, he could not stay. So, I had to convince him at times that he was a leader, especially when people were depending on you as a musician.

We traveled across the highways, to spend some time with his family during the holidays. That we would all be together.

My husband had a large family, so whenever we traveled to their city, it was for a week or more of stay because they all lived in the same area, and to me it was like going to another state although it was in California and 2 hours away. So, I had the opportunity of meeting his entire family and they were all sweetly saved, loved the Lord, and filled with the precious Holy Spirit. Well, many of them especially the female of the family. I was so glad because this enhanced my transformation and enriched my spiritual life. Whenever we visited the families "Church of God in Christ" at the time the Pastor was his uncle the late Pastor Conedy, on Sunday sometimes during the week but it was a family church, as the songwriter wrote it was a "Family Affair" for sure. I enjoyed this so much because, getting back to my musical abilities in church and where I needed to be at this time as

God was *transforming my life*. Sometimes I would attend with, Little George, with all his Aunties, Uncles, and cousins, as they spoiled him. Most of the time his daddy was always on the road as a Union musician but at most events, I would travel with him.

So now I am a part of the "Conedy family" who were well known in that part of the city, town, and state. Not knowing the enemy was on my trail for my husband, no one warned me. So that was a spiritual battle, well, I had to realize how we started and the relationship he was in and the lifestyle I was experiencing. But I believe God was in the works of this, bringing me back to the fold, as well as changing his life.

Now I am the directress of a choir and director of Youth and Young Adult with a baby. I must say all the young people at the Little Zion Missionary Baptist Church in Compton, Calif. worked together, as well as sang together.

BUT AS ALWAYS, the Devil tries to stop and block progress, but they knew how to fight as well as pray, if it wasn't through the young people, it was between musicians and me. But we would come together and bind up all the forces of the enemy, that was not like God. There were so many activities outside they participated. We always traveled to sing, of course, they were so anointed in their singing although' they were young people and acted it out just as we all do in our teen and young adult stages. But I was never disrespected as their leader by any, in fact, they enjoyed togetherness, and no one could come into their group uninvited. I was blessed to welcome parents to travel with us in support.

We sometimes traveled with the Adult Choir. At this church, there were so many who enjoyed singing at the time and we had so many activities. We had youth night, and skating, to keep them in church. There were so many age groups in the singing and music department we had to separate into many other choirs as the:

- The Voices of Zion
- Senior Choir
- Men Choir
- Rosebud
- Youth and Young Adult Choir

# PART FOUR
## Chapter Seventeen
# FROM PREPARATION TO TRANSFORMATION

Now God had begun to show himself strong and mighty in my life and lead me to my purpose as He began to transform me into what He desired. I had no idea of what was going on at the time and not knowing it began with new church life and my marriage and my new church family, and now all I wanted to do was serve God in the capacity I was experiencing and His way and not my way. I had little eyes (well not so little now) watching me every day all day and did not mine it at all. (my three girls)

So here we are, my new family and children, watching them grow at home and in the church as I mentioned. There were many activities for the young people at the "Little Zion Missionary Baptist Church" in the City of Compton California.

When my son was younger, he loved to sit at the organ with his daddy, I really thought He was going to be an Organist, but God bless his hand to play drums. His dad bought his first set of drums for Christmas and became a church drummer.

The adults enjoyed as well as the children because their children were involved as well as my husband George Conedy, although he had no parental skills, and neither did I. most of the events were musicals dramas, concerts, and plays.

As the late bro henry, the great gospel broadcaster) would say: *"what a time, what at time, what a good time"* there were so many talented, gifted, anointed young people in that church and this made it so much more exciting and motivational, and other young people would come and join because they enjoyed doing the lords work together and continue even in this time we lived in now.

There were street gangs, drugs, alcoholic gangs and so much they could have been involved but they chose to follow Jesus. there was a time when we were forced to wear certain colors so that we would not be identified with the street gangs, not to name any but I'm sure you are familiar with the gangs of Compton, cal. watts, and the others. but God kept us safe everywhere we traveled.

Things began to change in my life almost immediately. I began to be involved in the youth and young adult department, of course, I have young people of my own now, along with other adults' assistance and their children. Whenever we traveled in the area there was a young lady who was a yellow bus driver superintendent, she would motor the young people on the bus, to our events and it was so convenient. not only was she our bus driver but also would sing in her uniform and play tambourines, whatever, and wherever God wanted to use her, she was ready. This went on for years at a time and it was great fun and excitement, they all were like family as God planned for these young people. I loved them and admired them so much for their tenacity, they were determined to go forward in the lord and make a difference in that community.

Some of them grew older and began to sing in the mass choir, that's when we combined all (5) five choirs together.

8:00 am SERVICE and 11:00 am SERVICE

There were opportunities for each choir to sing at either both services or one, of course, my husband played for both services, which meant I had to be there with my family, and that meant changing my schedule at work of course, as I continued to work. because we needed that money. The children were growing up and needed more clothes and loved to eat and by this time little George, the baby, was walking, singing, and playing tambourines in the rosebud choir. very gifted, anointed, and talented, as his father, at an early age.

So, I began to work the night shift and come straight to church from work, then if I had to direct the choir, run home take a shower pick up my family prepare them, and be in the 8:00 AM service, for the processional of the choir. It was a delight, something I enjoyed with pleasure. Of course, many times I had to miss the 11:00 AM service for time to go home and prepare dinner, and be in bed early, of course when you are young, you have the energy to move about to and from.

We sang at special events, occasions, and church affairs, and had our own concerts for the young people and they love to dress in beautiful uniforms, and I love them to look beautiful and handsome. Especially whenever we visit other churches, we march into the choir stand it took 200 choir members a long time to march in as well as find room for all Of course, we looked good and sang great they enjoyed this part of it though I had our own children, they all became a part of my family and life.

# Chapter Eighteen
## (wisdom in transformation)
### *Steps to a Transformed Life*

When we are ready to give our all to the Lord, not withholding anything back, and when we open our spirit to receive, God will transform our lives and renew our mind from carnal worldly to the right Spiritual mind for Him.

*"Be transformed by the renewing of your mind" Romans 12:2*

We live out Gods will when we change our thoughts to Gods thoughts, rather than living like the world dictates.

**JUST A FEW SPIRITUAL STEPS**

**OF MY INITIAL TRANSFORMATION**

**AND HOW GOD MOVED IN AND**

**THROUGH MY LIFE.**

1. I had to give myself completely to God as a living sacrifice. God do not need dead, animal sacrifices in this day and time. Because of all HE has done and is doing for us.

   Remember while I was yet sinning, He died just for me, and it was His Grace and Mercy that kept me alive.

2. I had to be transformed by the truth, and not by man's opinions of the word, the way they think, and the way I think.

   Many times, we listen to what our friends, families, and others say, what they think and it's not the true word of God, with much error. We must study and read the word for ourselves inviting the Holy Spirit to speak.

3. I had to be realistic about myself, and not think that I am better than others during my change. As God was giving me spiritual insight. I was real and honest with evaluating myself by my faith in what I believe.

4. I used whatever gift I had been given to serve others to the best of my ability.

Remember your gift is not for you to use for your glory. WE must remember we are to serve each other with our gifts, and talents and to bring others to Gods kingdom, and to help them find their purpose in life. Your gift will make room for you and bring you among great men.

# Chapter Nineteen
## A Transformed Life

Jesus is the best thing that ever happened to me, and my family has grown up in size, age, and smart. but no more babies, we had enough to raise. and now we were trying to settle into our new apt. in Compton, this was closer for my son in Christian school when he had to learn to walk at his age. Then he graduated from Christian Foundation School which his family the Conedy supported for years, he was potty trained here which was favorable.

Then He graduated from the Christian Foundation and started in another Christian School because the public schools in Compton were not so great. So, I signed him in a Parochial Catholic School, "Our Lady of Victory" in Compton, California, until his dad decided he needed a taste of Public School, but when he decided to play hooky and walk home. Due to dirty bathrooms. I decided to use the predominantly Caucasian school for its safety, learning ability, and better area. It began to look better until the enemy tried to bring that suffered with acute asthma which kept him home most of the time until I received help from the school Then He graduated from the Christian Foundation and started in another Christian School because the public schools in Compton were not so great. So, I signed him in a Parochial Catholic School, "Our Lady of Victory" in Compton, California, until his dad decided he needed a taste of Public School, but when he decided to play hooky and walk home. Due to dirty bathrooms. I decided to use the predominantly Caucasian school for its safety, learning ability, and better area. It began to look better until the enemy tried to bring that suffered with acute asthma which kept him home most of the time until I received help from the school. where it was drug-infested and because my husband was a freelance musician, he became involved in some of the activities that were not welcomed, but because at the time we needed the finances, we did not know how to depend on the Lord, although I continued to work at the hospital. Years went by and we were still there. The area we lived in became very hostile and violent.

There came a time when sometimes we had to sleep on the floor to dodge the shootings that would occur in and around our street area. Waking up in the morning with bullet holes in the side of the house from gang violence, we tried a block Club and a quiet prayer walk but that did not work because no one was spiritual enough or had enough faith to continue if I must say. We decided it was time for us to move our family out of danger. We found a nice house in Compton a few blocks away but out of the danger zone.

Now that the Lord was growing me into the woman he created me to be, and there were women, in my circle, strong, spirit-filled, powerful, anointed black women around me, speaking into my life, to keep me on the straight and narrow way, there were so many times I wanted to become a spiritual leader helping other women to keep their mental and spiritual stability position as a woman and not allow men to control them. Then I found myself in this position but had the knowledge and strength to pull myself by the bootstrings. Well, I also wanted a perfect marriage with perfect children of course this may be every woman's desire and dream if not selfish concerning their lifestyle. What I mean by this, is we want whatever makes us happy, but darn if we know how sometimes, and then don't want to make others happy around us.

We are Women who are evolving every day, all the time, however, choosing what we want who we desire, how we desire and guess what? We get just what we want and desire in the flesh many times, although it is not in God's perfect will. So women here I am with a handsome husband, very popular in the City, beautiful children, a nice home, good paying job, working in the church, enjoying the people around the church and town and here comes the enemy in my life, supposedly to be a friend in church, trying to help her in her lifestyle but she, desires to destroy my marriage, through my husband as a musician, well everyone wanted the best and he was the best around town as a freelance musician, but at this time, I was too strong in the word and very strong in my own flesh, trying to do the right thing, but I still had some baggage's, and so did my husband, George, to work out in our marriage. He was very protective of me, because I was extremely attractive, dressed the best, and talented, musically inclined, and yes, he would let you know he had a beautiful wife, and people did not understand how I hooked up with him and his lifestyle. Well, I was in love now with my husband and he was in love with me, and we had children no one was going to get in between our marriage, regardless.

Now, I felt this was God sent to me. (My shining armor) In the beginning, I did have some doubts due to his circumstances not to mention he was on probation at the time coming out of drug addiction, selling drugs, just as I did in the past but, never got caught I believe God joined us together after his divorce maybe to lift our spirits. I just believe it was God's timing, for my first marriage and to raise a family.

As Paul states in Ephesians 4:22 to take off your former way of life, the old self that is corrupted by deceitful desires, to be renewed in the spirit of your mind, and to put on the new self, the one created according to God's likeness in righteousness and purity of the truth.

Well according to this scripture I was trying to take off my former way of living, the old lifestyle and live as Godly lifestyle, pure and righteous by the Grace of God, as much as humanly possibly women of God.

But some women in the church house just would not leave me and my family alone. Well God worked it out for me. He moved them out of the church. Thank God. Our marriage began to grow lovely and loving.

*"What God has joined together, let no one separate." Matt.19:6*

We began to work together in Ministry as a Family. My husband began to use his musical abilities in the Church and the Lord began to bless him to record his first *Christmas album*. Yes, there were albums in that century called George Conedy at the Hammond Organ Christmas. I was so proud of him, and he became extremely popular again around the Christmas Season, but I attended every concert and every service just to support him and in his presence. I will never forget my sister came out to visit, James Cleveland invited my husband to his church as a musician it was exciting for us to meet him in person. Of course, He was his organist on most of His records, and just to mention a few Johnsons Harrison and the L. A. Messengers, Los Angeles Choir, and many others. Also, my husband always had "GIGS" for weddings. I had the opportunity to meet great musicians, and my husband always wanted me to travel with him.

He became a musician for so many weddings, so we organized the wedding business, and ordered a caterer, because cooking was out of our (jurisdiction) we planned the wedding, and I sang, as He was the musician for a small fee at the time. But it paid some of our bills even though we had fun. That happened for a few years.

We traveled throughout Los Angeles, County, and sometimes flew to others because it was his job at the time, He was a union musician and whenever he was called, he would drive or fly. Opportunities for me to travel with him, of course, he didn't go, or would not go without me, (his wife). His first album was amazing and continues to be on social media.

We traveled with the church to Las Vegas, and although he had family there, we did not stay with them, it was our vacation/honeymoon. 1978. We had a wonderful marriage enjoying Church, our families, and friends.

# Chapter Twenty
## A New Life in Christ

God began to move in our lives as a family. Things began to move so quickly now that I am more settled in my mind and trying to wrap all this around my head about what the Lord was doing to my husband and me.

Since we did not have the opportunity for a real honeymoon, we decided to take a trip to the island in the States, called "Catalina Island" for a weekend, of course since we were the musicians in the church it was a short time, it was called the "Catalina Island" just across the ocean from Long Beach Calif. We boarded a ship to get there, close to where we lived.

Just some adventures of our married life, as we enjoyed each other and were allowed to use by God Yes, God began a new thing in my life, as I began to plan and work things out it was already worked out in His timing and His plans. Because my husband was such a great musician and I was trying to be the perfect (help meet) wife, and mother, when he traveled there, I was in the midst of it all. It was such a joy.

My transformation all happened so fast if I must say expeditiously and I was reaping the benefit of it all. Well as I said before we met in the flesh, but God turned it around for our good. I realize this is my story but most of it consists of my marriage with children life this was such an exciting time for everyone, watching my son grow into maturity and the girls as young ladies. As they begin to move forward in their adult life, attempting to train a child in the way they should go so when they are old, they will not depart. Well, we did not want them to depart from the church, the word of God or the family. But there comes a time when we must let them go.

Well, we inherited another son, (godson) to live with us, who was my Pastor's grandson, he stayed with us for a year or two, the girls grew and married so it was the 2 boys with us. This was LiL George's last year in High School, our godson was in grade school, so it appeared as though we were started over, but it did not last long. Our last girl decided to marry and move back home to save money for the wedding. Such a beautiful enjoyable time.

Then George was still in High School, at a new School in a New town, Paramount, close to home but far enough, as I stated before, the schools in Compton were not suitable at the time for my child. One more year and we would be free of all our children, I thought.

Well, George and my godson stayed with us for a while, and continued in church, if you lived in the Conedy home you were bound for church. That is what we did continuously, but they enjoyed it because as I aforementioned, there were many activities for our Young People, Skating, bowling, and even outings on the weekend. They loved church. We made it very enjoyable as they were taught the word of God.

There were so many talented young People. We had a playwriters, and many of them performed in the plays as we rented different theaters and Auditoriums to raise money for the Young People uniforms, etc. He would write the plays from Pastor Fisher's Sermons or something from the Holy Spirit. I will never forget John's first play; it was played so many times and "Back by Popular Demand" and all the youth were participants. This one I will never forget; He was friends with the late "Tommy Ford" they all went to school together with my nephew.

I began to get involved in Women Ministry, Noon Day Prayer, Sunday School, and Young People Ministry. This is where I began my spiritual growth in Ministry.

I always communicate and served with the older group of women, such as the Mother Board, and Deaconess. I will never forget, my Spiritual Mother, Mom Anderson trained me in Street Ministry and Outreach. Every Wednesday evening, we prepared meals for Skid row downtown Los Angeles, this was real ministry, we had a team of interested people not only to feed them physical food but also spiritual food afterwards in an apartment building, of the city. We brought blankets and cardboard boxes in the winter and clothes, food, and water in the summer. This prevented them from eating out of the trash can and sleeping on the cold cemented street/sidewalk, this was their lifestyle of living. I am speaking of me.

TRANSFORMED LIFE that the Lord saved for His purpose, to become His workman, and He would receive ALL THE GLORY.

*"For we are His workmanship, created in Christ Jesus for good works, which God prepared beforehand that we should walk in them."*
*Ephes.2:10*

*"For I know the plans I have for you" this is the Lord's declaration plans for your well-being, not for disaster, to give you a future and a hope." Jeremiah 29:11*

I believe it was many years, we were members of this church. (well, my son was born) from birth raised in the church, grew up in the church, we lived in the church every week,) and until he was old enough to spread his wings, yes, we kept him under our wings for a long time, that's all He knew was church (a church boy) He became the drummer in the church band and the young choir. I forgot to mention, that this was a Missionary Baptist Church and since my husband grew up in the Church of God in Christ, he played the organ with drums in the church, I suppose you can guess the other part, yes, he had to introduce drums to this Baptist Church, we attend, of course it was in the beginning when he introduce me to the church. But that was history of the "Little Mount Zion Missionary Baptist Church," but it had to be approved by the "Executive Board" of the church. Much different than now, as I write this portion of my drums are apart, of the church will not go on without drums in the music department. Things have changed in this Century.

This became a Growing, Spirit-filled, Church on the corner of Wilmington Blvd. in the City of Compton, California. It was a growing young church until you were sure to get there early either for a parking space or a seat in the congregation. Although. There were two services, Sunday Mornings at 8:00 and 11:00 of course during Anniversaries, Conventions, and Holidays, it was so exciting to me at the time because it began to remind me a little bit of Community Baptist in Atlantic City, my home church. But I began to really get excited about the word, we studied every Wednesday evening taught by the Deacons of the church and more bible study of the word. which I did not make it applicable to myself at home, in Atlantic City. As the Older folk say I was in the church, but the church was not in me. I never heard the word Salvation. This was the beginning of my Salvation, relationship with the Lord as Jesus planned.

I was learning the word, also developing spiritual growth with the women ministries we also visit and fellowship with other women ministries throughout Compton and Los Angeles. But much of my time was learning the word and singing in the Choir, directing the choir, learning new songs, Music programs afternoon services but somehow the word of God was being imparted in my life for learning.

# Chapter Twenty-One
## A Difficult Task

*"The thief cometh not, but to steal, kill and destroy. -John 10:10*

A few years passed by so fast, my husband and I were getting to a difficult stage in our life, where he was doing more than I expected for the world than for the Lord and this took a change in our lifestyle of living. His music was not going in the direction I wished it would go. I guess because he did not depend on the Lord, we were leaning to our own understanding, and not listening and adhering to what the Lord was saying to us. So, we began to have a little struggle with our marriage which resulted in separation. By this time, my son was still with me and continued to stay in church and participate in the Young Adult Department. My husband decided to leave this church and use his music in worldly events. But God had begun to work on me and keep me focused, I was determined not to allow the world but the word, to lead my life, and I was pleased with what he was doing. Now I am ready to "get it on a popping" and see what the Lord has instore for me in ministry. After we left the church in Compton they led my husband to another church in Inglewood, another Baptist called Little Light Ministries, wherever he went in Jesus' Name I would follow him, this was a little storefront church in the back street, but good preaching, sweet family church, and the people were churchgoers there every Sunday just and a hand full of us and my husband was the Organist. So here I became the choir director, assisting with the music department and the women ministry. Then I picked us something different, the youth Praise dancer, and taught praise dance which I had never ever experienced in the

Baptist church, but the Pastors daughter and young people were interested, so I took them under my wings and again it was on "a Poppin" we continued that for years, I also took them to a Praise and Worship Symposium lead by a friend I met where they would learn the biblical history, of Praise and Worship and were trained. I was a member here for about 5 or 6 years, but my husband left, and I didn't like how he dismissed himself, so I stayed on and became the Church pianist and formed a choir, along with the praise and worship team with the help and strength of the Lord. We began to have musicals, and concerts invited the different churches in the area, and one of the famous singers, we knew was our guest singer and also, the First Lady knew Stevie Wonder through her brother, and we did not announce it, but he just made an appearance, not the special guest.

Then, I became 50 years young and had my 50th Birthday Musical Celebration, inviting all the choirs and Churches I ever sang or played the piano. It was a great and first-ever Celebration, at this time all I wanted to do was to serve, God and minister to him in Praise and Worship. So I was there for a few years, and my journey continued as my husband continued in different areas of Los Angeles, I tried to follow him as his supportive and loving wife. The enemy began his tricks in my marriage and began to build strongholds, and in his mind, listening to people and not the voice of the holy spirit, we began to have difficulties in our home and in our marriage, allowing the enemy to play havoc in his mind, due to the lust of the world in his music and lifestyle changes.

Strongholds can cause us to think in ways that block us from God's best. When we conform to worldly lust and not transform our minds by renewing with the word of God, the enemy wreaks havoc in our ministry, marriage, and family and delays our purpose and assignment. Well, I had a made-up mind, and determined to run on to see what the end was going to be. I did not

This is what happens in our marriages when we allow the enemy to take control, and the other person gets out of control. I was dedicated to the work of the Lord, committed to his promises and assignment for me, and the other, allows obey the world, and not the word, it began to be frazzle, dazzle, it began to appear as though we were unequally yoke together, when I knew different, because of his religious background and family. He was saved, and baptized in the water but did not have a relationship with the Lord.

*"Be not conformed to the pattern of this world but be transformed by the renewing of your mind" Romans 12:2*

I pursued or encouraged him to get baptized at the church we attend as a family. L.Z.M.B.C. Now, don't get me wrong, he loves the Lord and has a god-fearing heart and love for the Lord as we all did at one time in our lives, some it takes longer to develop a relationship. A great Musician in the City of Los Angeles, very much anointed and gifted always in demand, but sometimes people will use your gift if you allow it. This happens with my husband and as a wife not being able to help in that department, just caring for our children.

This was a difficult task, not hard but difficult when two are not agreeing and not knowing how to settle disagreements without counseling, ignoring appointments for counseling attempting to settle. When your friends, families, or others are going through situations and difficulties, and need counseling, there is no need to receive assistance from them, because we are adding fuel to the fire going into a blind spot and into darkness again.

Only God can and will work it out for you because He knows all and sees all, that's where "lean not to your own understanding; we must acknowledge Him, know that he is all-knowing, omniscient, and He knew what's best for our marriage because it was a spiritual battle and we had to learn how to pray with each other and teach our children how to pray.

This was difficult for me to work in the kingdom under this type of pressure in my marriage, But I would feel the Holy Spirit tugging on my spirit to stay in the safety zone and get it right although my other half was struggling with his demons and his religiosity. I had to continue to move ahead toward the goal in my purpose which God had prepared for me. It's difficult when you have a family now and keeping the family focus, you are trying to wear a skirt and pants, (that's just a cliché) because we as women cannot be fathers to our sons, therefore we do not wear pants in the household, only try to be the mother and wife and show them the right way in just being that example by living the lifestyle of a godly woman. Even with the girls everyone attended church in the Conedy's house as a family, regardless of what negativity the enemy would try to throw at me.

So here we are separated in churches and in marriage, trying to live a lifestyle as the Christian in the family for our children. But God had his hands on us because we were children of the King, trying to live a godly life. I believe He was behind the scenes working thing out for our good. I believe this, so knowing there were praying women around in my city I began to get involved in the prayer group and watch God do His thing in my life and in my home. The women began to pray with me and for my household, and God began to move in our lives. The enemy tried it each time, there were so many difficulties, more downs and lows, than ups, and highs, but I never gave in nor gave up. God had plans for me in ministry and I was ready to pursue whatever God had for me.

Thank God for Revelation knowledge to guide me into the beginning of the work in his kingdom. I did not have revelation knowledge in the beginning of where or what God was doing these scriptures led me in my walk and my journey of Transformation and my identity in the Lord.

What no eye has seen, nor ear heard, nor the heart of man imagined what God has prepared for those who love him.

*Philippians 1:6*
*And I am sure of this, that he who began a good work in you will bring it to completion at the day of Jesus Christ.*

*Ephesians 3:20*
*Now to him who is able to do far more abundantly than all we ask or think, according to the power at work within us.*

Thank God for the Holy Spirit and my obedience to listen and continue in the work of the kingdom as the Lord began my transformation in my life. Many times, God will do things in your life we are not aware of what he is doing but, by the function of Holy Spirit, it happens.

*Ephesians 2:10*
*For we are his workmanship, created in Christ Jesus for good work, which God prepared ahead of time for us to do.*

*Ephesians 1:18*
*I pray that the eyes of your heart may be enlightened so that you may know what the hope of his calling is, what is the wealth of his glorious inheritance in the saints, and what is the immeasurable greatness of his power toward us who believe according to:*

Isaiah 62:2

You shall be called by a new name, which the mouth of the Lord shall name.

Philippians 4:13

I can do all things through Christ who gives me strength.

I John 3:1

See what great love the father has lavished on us.

# Chapter Twenty-Two
## A New Identity

*2 Corinthians 5:15*

*And he died for all so that those who live should no longer live for themselves, but for the one who died for them and was raised.*

Therefore, if anyone is in Christ, he is a new creation, the old has passed away, and see the new has come!

I began to read the Jabez Prayer, and others to stabilize my mind and yield to the Holy Spirit in my marriage and allow God to do it, not me and my husband. Whenever your life is in shambles everyone and everything around you will follow this pattern, but when we take our hands off the situation and really say "God I am in your hands" and truthfully desire in your heart, this will begin to move and change.

I had begun to recognize my new identity in Christ, a New Creation, a new personality, a new start and a new person in marriage not trying to fix it on my own. So, I learned that Jesus liberates us from sin and its dominating power and restores us to a new relationship with Him. Where we are free to no longer live for ourselves but for him who died for me and rose for me to have abundant life in my home and marriage.

So, when I realize His transforming love compels me to live with a new identity and purpose, it helps me to look at my life differently and help to lead other women into their purpose. But it was not easy for me, I realized my marriage was my ministry and my husband was my number one ministry. As I began to look forward to the purpose of my life it was identified with Christ and the church. We are the church and Jesus is coming back for His Church. (Marriage) I hope this is understood in your marriage or before you marry. It is not easy when God joins you together with your mate, spouse, or husband, we are no longer (twain) 2 as the bible speaks but (one) but recognizing who you are in Christ has one hundred percent to add to it for a healthy marriage.

It helps us to point others to Jesus, and it's much easier to point and help others to our Savior, the one who can make them new people, know their identity in Christ, become who He desires of us as one body, or as one in marriage as your discovery your New Identity in Him. "Now you are a new creation to lead others to him, not alone but together with my husband as Jesus led us to the right path. Because we lean not to our own understanding.

"Lean not to your own understanding but acknowledge His ways and He will direct your path."

I know this to be absolutely manifest in my new identity in Christ, so many times, I did not know who or what I was doing until I learned to learn and depend on Jesus.

I pray this helps someone at this moment in their life to find Christ inside and to strengthen the inner man to help them with their walk with Christ in their purpose, ministry, home, marriage, church, occupation, career wherever there is a need for Transformation and your New Identity.

Once this change takes place in our lives, (let me speak for myself,) in my life there is no going back, because I have been moved forward to making a difference in my life and getting all the nicks and crannies out of my marriage, putting forth the effort to save my marriage for my children. Although it was hard, God helped us through it all.

Because we lean and depend on Him: Because He Is me.

- Jehovah Jireh: My provider Gens 22:14

- Jehovah Rapha: My Healer. Exodus 15:26

- Jehovah Nissi Reign Exodus 17:15

- Jehovah Raah: My Shepherd Psalm 23:1

- Jehovah Shalom: My Peace in the middle of the storm. Judges 6:24

- Jehovah Shammah: the Lord is present Ezekiel 48"35

- Jehovah Tshikeneu: The Lord our Righteousness Jeremiah. 23:6

Without this prayer, or without calling His name and the presence of Him in my life, there is no way I could do without Him.

# Chapter Twenty-Three
# Comfort Zone

## A New Beginning

*Ask what you desire, and it shall be done for you. By this My Father is glorified that you bear much fruit; so, you will be My disciples."*
*John 15:7-8*

As time continued to move on and I continued to procrastinate concerning my purpose for my desire now was to do God's will no turning back to nonsense chaos, and stupidity of life. First, I Had to step out of my comfort Zone This was now my New Identity, My New beginning entering and becoming My transformation of Life.

Now I had no idea, nor understood how and what God was going to orchestrate my life, to change. I knew what my feelings were, although it was not about my feelings, it was about God being glorified as I bear fruit with my life. As I read "Enlarge my territory" Jabez prayer, I thought about how my territory can be enlarged when there is no more room in my life for enlargement, I can't handle this moment. God was preparing me for something I could not handle before now. I was moving at a slow pace in assignments and in my position with no bible training, but the bible also mention that if you are willing.

*"God is able to do exceeding and abundantly above all that we can ask or imagine, but according to His power within us." Ephes. 3:20*

We all have a comfort zone that we nurture, feed into and hold on for dear life, well that was me, I was fearful of stepping out, But

I read "if you want to claim God's best for you, don't plan on spending too much time in your present comfort zone".

I was so comfortable in the status quo or in singing in the choir, and directing the choir because it was just moving from smaller to larger but still in the same space afraid of acquiring more "territory" in my life. I was afraid of "what if" or "if I do this" the cycles of being comfortable, or discomfort, and moving from here to there with the same old same old, if you know what I mean, going around in circles and cycles.

Let me try to break it down as "Dr. Bruce Wilburn in "Jabez" he says:

**COMFORTNESS**, you have feelings of rest and security when going to occupy your territory, but with God's help, we see a Mountain we can move out of our way.

**DISCOMFORT**, your feelings of fear kick in because you are overwhelmed and want to go backward from the new challenge. But God helps us to take courage and take that Mountain, "I CAN" And then.

**BACK IN COMFORT**, we feel great, exhilarated, excited about the new task, and new ministry as we move forward, greater faith, and thankful about it.... but then, excitement leaves and right back in our comfort zone.

It happened repeatedly, to me, as I tried to move forward in my purpose, and the plans for my life because I tried to do it on my own. I allowed fear to stop me, and God was trying to grow and lead me in my Gifted Calling for Him, but I kept moving from comfort to discomfort cycles, really trying to please my flesh and other people thinking I could do it on my own. But as fear came in, I thought it was God saying NO this is not it, but it was my flesh getting in the way of what I could do if I trusted in God and leaned not on my own understanding.

Sometimes we must run to that Lion discomfort zone say: "Lord here am I" I am ready and watch him come with bigger ministry with courage and strength. God keeps his promise to us, if He said it, He would do it, we must listen wait and then step out on faith and do it.

*"His strength is made perfected in our weakness, when we are weak, He is strong...." 2 Corinthians 12:9-10*

My biggest desire was to learn and receive as much from and for the Lord, teach and share what I received. My heart was now open to the knowledge and wisdom of God, so I suppose He was trying to enlarge my territory but because I was in my comfort zone, it felt as if God was nudging me to continue in what I was involving myself. In all the churches I attended and serviced, I learned things other than music, such as singing in the choir and being music director, along with retaining my home position as a wife and mother. God was speaking to me to move forward to something bigger than me.

A New beginning, this was all new to me other than my marriage to my sweet handsome adorable husband, it was different, and with my guy, it was exciting in all of this. He introduced me to the church where we ministered. We make our plans, but God interrupts and determines our steps, as the bible states in Proverbs 16:9 the heart of man plans his ways, but the LORD establishes his steps."

I can plan every aspect of my life, but God is the only one who decides what will happen. This is what I have been doing with my life, and nothing seems to work for me because it was not the plans God had for me, He might had permitted my desire with some but, not with all. So, this is a new beginning for me and my family, finally, it is coming together. We both had a gift God entrusted us with but what were our plans with this gift? We must use it not for the world but for our creator and allow it so that others would be blessed. In all of this, even my son was a blessing as a musician, my girls were just supporters, no special talent there. But this time it was about my husband and his son working together in the church and sometimes it was all three as in some of the pictures you can see. Such a blessing. There were times I did not know how to appreciate how the Lord Blessed my family at that time, I suppose it was too early or we were too young and did not understand the narrative of it all.

But the Lord steps in and takes control of His gift He has entrusted us with so that He may receive Glory. In this new beginning from the Lord, He gave us the power to move on and press on to higher heights in Him as we began to trust in the Lord and lean not to our own understanding, but acknowledge his way, so He directed our path, gave us a new beginning in our marriage and music career. We began to travel as a family spreading the music ministry, yes, I would travel with Him as God began to bless us in our finances, as well as in our home as we really needed.

As I continued to read and study the Jabez Prayer book, God would show me my purpose in him and move me toward my goal in Him. L joined a women's prayer group and began to grow stronger in the Lord as I participated and became serious about my spiritual walk with the Lord.

I began to assist other women in this church and learn more about my life in the Transformation of my journey. The Lord began to strengthen me as His Chosen Vessel as I gave more of myself to him allowing Him to move me into a greater thing. I began to see visions of where he was leading me and just allow him to use me even in my weakness, He made me strong because it was not I but the Christ moving inside me, or should I say the Holy

Spirit as I opened myself and allowed him to use me. I didn't have much time to do everything needed on my schedule, not enough hours in the day, and days in the week it seemed as though there was no time for me. My schedule began to be so busy.

As I read in the book (Jabez) it began to live in my spirit. God will arrange circumstances and opportunities that are more strategic for you he began to do it for me. I didn't get more hours in my days, I just found more effective ways of using the hours that were given to me. That made sense to me, so I found the time as God gave me the work, after I realized who my employer was and who I was working for and what I was working with.

*"For we are His workmanship, created in Christ Jesus for good works, which God has prepared beforehand that we should walk in them."*
*Ephesians 2:10.*

God showed me how he wanted to use me as His workmanship, a chosen vessel to work for Him in ministry, so I decided to follow Jesus and do it His way, and not my way and then he began to open doors in ministry and financially. When we allow God to do it His way, and realize we are His employees and not men, that's when He turns things around for our good and for His Glory. So, this is my new beginning, my New Journey, the New Ministry of my TRANSFORMATION LIFE.

# Chapter Twenty-Four
# God's Chosen Vessel

*"But the Lord said to him, "Go for he is a chosen vessel of Mine to bear My name before Gentiles, Kings, and the children of Israel "*
Acts 9:15

- A chosen Vessel has been created for a specific purpose.
- A person called by God and who He uses as His vessel.
- Leaders God called and equipped for His service and His Glory.

Characteristics a chosen vessel possesses:

- Can be used, even with flaws.
- A chosen vessel is filled.
- A chosen vessel pours out.
- A chosen vessel is holy.

For reasons known only to Him, God has chosen to work through men and women who are willing to make sacrifices for the sake of the "thing" He has placed in their hearts to do. Andy Stanley

Some years now had passed and during this time in my life my husband and I had separated, and we moved on in our lives, but we continue to communicate. I still had my baby, son with me as God use us in ministry together for a while. Then my husband became ill, and my son went to live with him until God called him home. Which was a sad moment, it was unexpected, so we had to prepare for that. But when I was called to the ministry of Jesus Christ, I really thought God did not like me at all, or He was punishing me for something. There was so much I experienced, such as living alone for a while then I found myself selling most of my furniture, giving it away, and living in my car for a moment, homeless for a few months or more, then there was a time when I was living in a women's center, as I mentioned in a few chapters. Called

**"God's House of Love"** with women from all walks of life, living and ministering in the same room. I talked to the Lord about and spoke in my spirit I had to know the hearts of the women who I minister to learning their heart's desire. This was before I was ordained as an Elder. So, I met the Ladies who prayed for me, supported me and led me to a spirit-filled church where I decided to attend **Bethany Bible College in Los Angeles, California to enhance and learn more** of the bible the right way. Graduated in 2002. Then my car broke down had to ride the bus from work to school and back home. I was blessed with a bus ministry, as part of my calling and Journey. where I ministered on the bus until everyone who was to be saved received it. Then that's when I was blessed with a new car and more ministry as His Chosen Vessel. God chose me to minister on the streets of Los Angeles downtown skid row I believe I spoke of that in my earlier chapters. This was all a part of my calling, a chosen vessel by God. I attended the International foursquare church School of Ministry, where I became Pastor of Music Ministry and New Members classes. Then attended Bethany Bible College. During this time in my life, God continued to place ministry before me, I became a radio broadcaster for women's prayer ministry on one of the Prestige's radio stations in Los Angeles Calif. Every Wednesday night ministered to women across the Nation as they would call in for Prayer. This was bigger than me so I as my team of women to assist me in prayer on the Phone.

After graduating from bible college, the Lord led me to another church called "The Anointed Ministries" leader Bishop Morris, where I attended the school of Ministry and was ordained as an Elder, never knew what an Elder consisted of until I attended this School of Ministry and began to teach and later lead Praise and Worship along with the First Lady and other Elders of the church.

I believe I was chosen and called by God for a specific purpose. But it was not until I developed a strong, intimate relationship with the Lord and decided to follow Him and Him only. Give up the worldly things and try Him with no other help but the Holy Spirit. This is when I was called to organize the Women Ministry in my Condominium.

This was after I gave up everything and being obedient to the voice of God. I had to sell all my possessions, which resulted in sleeping in my car some nights, too much pride to as tell my friends at the time, but when my friends found out they were so supportive, but this is because I was chosen by God as His Vessel of Honor, and it was not an easy task. This was a long, lonely road I had to travel. During this time, as I said in the previous chapter how the Lord called me to radio ministry and then called me to a Women ministry for Lady Elect. This was remarkably interesting for me being that I was never a lady Elect but God prepared me for the task of ministering to these women who were hurting, broken, battered, physically and spiritually abused. So, as His chosen Vessel, he prepared me for this ministry. I believe it was because of my marriage, and my past lifestyle, also what and how he delivered me. There were so many exciting events, women's conferences, retreats, and learning institutes for me to attend and become a member.

Through all of this, God was still calling me to ministry for women to help their deliverance from drugs, alcohol, abusive relationships, and other situations. Before my husband was deceased a few years later my son had decided to marry, and my husband was to be his best man. As we planned at the wedding planning party.

# Chapter Twenty-Five
## *The Calling*

"GOD DOES NOT CALL THE QUALIFIED,

HE QUALIFIES THE CALLED"

Jesus does not call the qualified; rather he qualifies the called. Calling the unqualified has always been God's specialty, if I might say; We can look at some of the heroic(sheroes) people of our past in the bible. Esther Ruth Miriam Deborah, Lydia, Abraham, Moses, Paul, and the list goes on and on. So, we must continue to step out in faith embracing the Lord's calling upon our lives and trusting him to guide us every step of the way, knowing; "All My help comes from the Lord the Maker of heaven and earth" (Psalm 121:1)

We must realize that we have been purchased at a price and redeemed by His blood. "He saved us and called us to a holy calling, not because of our works but because of his own purpose and grace. 2 Timothy 9

And we know that all things work together for good to them who are called according to their purpose. Rom. 8:28

Prayer: Lord empowers and strengthens us to walk out our Holy calling for you.

In this phase of my ministerial assignment, God called out one ministry for women called "Weaker Vessel Women Ministry International" siting at my table in my Condo before my transformation period. A few of the Ladies around the table helped me organize the Women ministry as we met once time a month and visited women's shelters and downtown missions for women in downtown Los Angeles, just to name a few ministries the Lord qualified and called as an assignment. Then I was qualified as an

Elder and called to preach. So, this was the beginning of my transformation. I remained in ministry for a few years or more until I retired from Harbor UCLA Medical Center. In 2006. Of course, there is more to this story, but I must continue at another time in another book. In my return home after retirement. This was a grand occasion and a beautiful event for my son and his fiancée.

We are in our state of preparation for my son's wedding at this sad time, missing my husband. A few days before Thanksgiving in 2006 with mixed emotions, although part of my New Jersey family will be coming out to the wedding. We will celebrate at Maria Calendars restaurant for Thanksgiving, such a joyous time with family from California also, as I prepare to return home to New Jersey, as planned.

I am having mixed emotions about returning home. But I did receive a call from the pastor in New Jersey to Pastor the Women ministry at that Particular church, Mount Zion Baptist Church, in Pleasantville New Jersey. We will talk more on my return home after 40 years in California, in the next book.

Now that I am officially in my calling, my assignment purpose by God and qualified by God to do work for my gift I can move forward to my New Jersey Assignment. But I must have a made-up mind when my son returns from their honeymoon, concerning my return home, to New Jersey.

This was the completion of my transformation and how the Lord will Prepare you for the Journey as He Qualified your call and sets your assignment leading you to His transformation life.

Even now I fell back into my comfort zone, as I prepared for my return. But God stepped in and gave me the courage I needed to move forward. Although I was in DESPERATION, it was all in the PREPARATION, and it became MY TRANSFORMATION

God was waiting on me, to change my mind, about my worldly ways, so that he could change the spirit man inside me.

Sometimes we think there has been a transformation in our lives once we have received the Lord Jesus Christ, don't get me wrong something takes place in our lives if we are open to receive. Until I was ready to receive, there was no renewed, restored, revitalized, process to take place. God continues to show me how I still need deliverance, discipline and transformation and it was evident in my life, regardless of how we excel in positions, titles, success and new job achievements, blessings of our own. We first must be real to ourselves in our Christian walk, and honor God in our substance in everything. We belong to him, and we were bought with a price. My life is not my own. Everything I have, everything has, all my possessions belong to him. "HAD IT NOT BEEN FOR THE LORD WHO WAS ON MY SIDE."

I pray you were blessed and have enjoyed reading my Story of transitioning, and transformation as much as I enjoy writing and sharing it with you. Many people see us in another light or mind and speak of what they thought she was well now you know, and I have never tried to be more than what God planned or had for me. I am what I am, who I am, an open book, nothing hiding because when you try to hide your sin God will expose you under that cover. So, we need to be a blessing to others by sharing our stories and stop hiding our sins, you are not an asset to others needing help in their walk with God.

So many people commit suicide, kill others, and are depressed trying to fit in and because of what people perceive they should be or define them as. But we hid behind the bible, the Cloth, our Choir Robes, preaching teaching, apostle, Evangelist, and whatever we call ourselves. I am so *glad I heard the voice of the Lord* and *hardened not my heart* to the obedience of his voice.

Transformed and delivered me.

- From a mess to his messenger

- From misery to ministry

- From a worldly, carnal Christian, to saved, Holy Ghost filled Women of God

- From the drug house to the Church house

- From homeless to the home of my own

- From the pit of darkness to His marvelous light

- From angry mad **BLACK** women to a humble sweet Christian woman.

- From a worldly church girl to a fiery spoken word woman of God.

- From a mistress to His minister.

GOD TURNED MY DARKNESS TO DAYLIGHT MY TRAGEDY TO TRIUMPH AND MY PREPARATION TO TRANSFORMATION.

# A Living Sacrifice
# (Wisdom in Transformation)

Therefore, I urge you, brothers, and sisters, in view of God's mercy, to offer your bodies as a living sacrifice, holy and pleasing to God—this is your true and proper worship. Do not conform to the pattern of this world but be transformed by the renewing of your mind. Then you will be able to test and approve what God's will is—his good, pleasing, and perfect will. Roman 12: 1-3

The song came to my mind.

"THE STRUGGLE IS OVER" WHAT NEXT?

# Acknowledgements

DEACONESS LOUISE NEBLETT

Thank you for your untiring, dedicated effort and assistance with my emergency, as my reader. You are such an asset as well as a blessing to People in the Kingdom of God. and Mount Zion Baptist Church, Women's Ministry, President

Rev. Shelly Williams
Pleasantville, New Jersey


The Late Pastor Jerome Fisher and the Late Lady Norma Fisher of Little Zion Baptist Church of Compton, California, (Greater Zion)


Pastor J. Hayes, and Lady Brenda Hayes
Little Light Baptist Church (Little Light Ministries)
Los Angeles, California.


Pastor Gwendolyn Hood, Pastor Johnnie Muck, and Jesse Lee III, Sr. Pastor of The International Church of The Foursquare Gospel
Los Angeles, California.


The Late Bishop John F. Morris and Lady Elect Hyacinth Morris of International Anointed Ministries, and Church
Los Angeles, California

My God daughters, of Compton, California
Pastor Karin Foster
Minister Nellie Mckinley
Jearlena Isrel

And the Little Zion Baptist Church Youth and Young Adults, of Compton, California

**CREDITS TO:**

H. Jackson Brown Jr.

John Dewey

Steve Nash

Book Celebration of Discipline
by Richard F. Foster
Donald Coggan: Quotes

MLK Transforming Center:
Martin Luther King Jr. Love Quote